EASY GRAMMAR PLUS WORKBOOK

Wanda C. Phillips

ISHA ENTERPRISES, INC.
Scottsdale, Arizona

© 1995

ISBN 0-936981-14-8

PREPOSITIONS:

about	down	throughout
above	during	to
across	except	toward
after	for	under
against	from	underneath
along	in	until
amid	inside	up
among	into	upon
around	like	with
at	near	within
atop	of	without
before	off	
behind	on	
below	onto	
beneath	out	
beside	outside	
between	over	
beyond	past	
but (meaning except)	regarding	
by	since	
concerning	through	

		FREE		

Name_____ **PREPOSITIONS**

Date_____

Directions: Unscramble the following prepositions.

1. twih-_____
2. stap-_____
3. ta-_____
4. nagol- a_____
5. fof-_____
6. no-_____
7. duren- u_____
8. nagasit- a_____
9. denboy- be_____
10. toni- in_____
11. mrof-_____
12. ot-_____
13. nithwi-_____
14. tebewen-_____
15. foereb-_____
16. socasr- a_____
17. pu-_____
18. boeva-_____
19. diam-_____
20. wolbe-_____

21. ethuneadnr-_____
22. tluin- u_____
23. wnod-_____
24. rane-_____
25. fro-_____
26. ni-_____
27. dibneh- b_____
28. nupo-_____
29. tthouiw-_____
30. tafre- a_____
31. darnou- af_____
32. goman- am_____
33. beedis-_____
34. ringdu-_____
35. vroe-_____
36. theeabn- b_____
37. gotuhrh- th_____
38. ubato- a_____
39. poat-_____
40. tub-_____

3

Name_____

Date_____

Directions: Unscramble the following prepositions.

1. yb- _by_____

2. uto- _out_____

3. dinesi- _inside_____

4. egninrcnoc- _concerning_____

5. petcex- _except_____

6. kiel- _like_____

7. fo- _of_____

8. deotuis- _outside_____

9. cines- _since_____

10. drwtao- _toward_____

11. gindrager- _regarding_____

12. oouuhhttgr- _throughout_____

4

nv
running

A PREPOSITIONAL PHRASE BEGINS WITH A PREPOSITION AND ENDS WITH A NOUN OR PRONOUN. That noun or pronoun is called the object of the preposition.

after dinner

(*after* is the preposition)
(*dinner* is the object of the preposition)
(*after dinner* is the prepositional phrase)

without you

(*without* is the preposition)
(*you* is the object of the preposition)
(*without you* is the prepositional phrase)

PREPOSITIONAL PHRASES WILL NOT BE THE SUBJECT OR VERB OF THE SENTENCE. (This holds true 99% of the time.)

SUBJECTS:

After crossing out all prepositional phrases, find **who** or **what** the sentence is about.

A. The man with his son walked toward me.

The man ~~with his son~~ walked ~~toward me~~.

B. Some of the ducklings waddled past us.

Some ~~of the ducklings~~ waddled ~~past us~~.

C. A book of stamps lay on the table.

A book ~~of stamps~~ lay ~~on the table~~.

VERBS:

After finding the subject of the sentence, decide **what happens/happened** or **what is/was** in the sentence. Remember: *The verb will never be in a prepositional phrase.*

A. The man ~~with his son~~ walked ~~toward us~~.

B. Some ~~of the ducklings~~ waddled ~~toward us~~.

C. A book ~~of stamps~~ lay ~~on the table~~.

6

Name_____ **PREPOSITIONS**

Date_____

Directions: Cross out any prepositional phrases. Underline the subject once and
the verb twice.

1.   The shoppers went into the store.

2.   A blender fell on the floor.

3.   We walked between the aisles of the supermarket.

4.   During the storm we held onto the side of the boat.

5.   Outside our home a pine tree grows.

6.   He stepped behind the door.

7.   The vacationers went to Disneyland.

8.   Throughout the day the rain came in the window.

9.   The price of soda is over a dollar.

10.   Past the large sign is a windmill.

11.   The report concerning smoking is in my desk.

12.   All students except Willie rode to school on a bus.

13.   The child went up the ladder and down the slide.

14.   The lettuce is inside the refrigerator by the milk carton.

15.   After the television program about snakes, we rode on our bikes to the zoo.

7

Name_____

Date_____

Directions: Cross out any prepositional phrases. Underline the subject once and
              the verb twice.

1.   After school we walked to the library.

2.   Mary sits behind you in science class.

3.   The plane flew above the clouds.

4.   Jane lives across the street from me.

5.   Down the road galloped the horse.

6.   We went to the beach.

7.   Some boys crawled under the car.

8.   The pump is behind the barn.

9.   They stopped along the road for five minutes.

10. During skiing season our family went to a lodge for a weekend.

11. The cars travel below the river and through the tunnel.

12. The telephone rang in the middle of the night.

13. Below the sink is the garbage can.

14. Everyone except Mary left by noon.

15. Within ten minutes of the call, my dad arrived in our driveway.

8

Name_____   **PREPOSITIONS**

Date_____

Directions: Cross out any prepositional phrases. Underline the subject once and
the verb/verb phrase twice.

Remember: Sometimes the preposition will have a compound object.

1.   We take our vacation in July and August.

2.   The gift was from John and his sister.

3.   The ball rolled between the chair and the sofa.

4.   In the spring or summer, I visit our friends for a week.

5.   The librarian gave the books to Tom and me.

6.   The meal of steak and potatoes was eaten at our favorite diner.

7.   The taxi driver left without his change or a tip from the passsenger.

8.   That good reader likes stories about horses and reptiles.

9.   Down streets and alleys trotted the owner in search of his lost pet.

10. During a trip to the zoo, the child stared at the lions and the tigers.

11. Above the door and windows was a shelf for plants.

12. All friends but Susan and Bill came to the party.

13. The band leader returned within five or ten minutes.

14. Before lunch and dinner the parent reads to the children.

15. Beyond the Earth and its moon are other planets.

List of helping verbs:

do
does
did

has
have
had

is
am
are
was
were
be
being
been

may
must
might
should
could
would
shall
will
can

There sometimes is a <u>compound subject</u> in a sentence. Compound subject means there are two or more subjects in the sentence.

A. During the snow storm, the boys and girls rushed home.

   ~~During the snow storm~~, the <u>boys</u> and <u>girls</u> rushed home.

B. Neither my <u>dad</u> nor my <u>mother</u> went to Mexico City.

   Neither my <u>dad</u> nor my <u>mother</u> went ~~to Mexico City~~.

C. Ms. Jones, Mr. Raimo, and Mrs. Burnhart will be in the office from nine until five.

   <u>Ms. Jones</u>, <u>Mr. Raimo</u>, and <u>Mrs. Burnhart</u> will be ~~in the office from nine until five~~.

Name_____ **PREPOSITIONS**
                                       Compound Subjects

Date_____

Directions: Cross out any prepositional phrases. Underline the subject once
               and the verb/verb phrase twice.

1.   Outside the building, the cats and dogs played.

2.   The burglar and his helper walked toward me.

3.   The broken cup and saucer were under the table.

4.   Milk or juice came with the meal.

5.   Up the tree scurried a squirrel and a chipmunk.

6.   Across the Golden Gate Bridge sped the cars and trucks.

7.   Neither my hand nor my foot hurt after the injury.

8.   My cousin and her roommate moved across the hall to a larger apartment.

9.   Within a week the detective and the other police officer solved the crime.

10.   Gloria and Robert married underneath the elm in our backyard.

11.   After the fire in our home, friends and neighbors came with boxes.

12.   Knives and forks were in the drawer under the counter.

13.   On the entryway table are a candle and a plant.

14.   The teacher and the principal talked about geography.

15.   For breakfast, cereal, pancakes, and toast were served.

<u>NOT is never a verb</u>. Do not underline NOT as part of the verb phrase.

    A. The <u>child</u> ~~with the red hair~~ <u>did</u> not <u>sit</u> ~~beside me~~.

    B. <u>He should</u> not <u>have given</u> his comb ~~to me~~.

    C. This <u>house</u> <u>is</u> not ~~for sale~~.

Date_____

Directions: Cross out any prepositional phrases. Underline the subject once and the verb/verb phrase twice.

Reminder: Not is an adverb. Do not underline NOT as part of the verb.

1. The swimmers were not competing for ribbons.

2. In the afternoon the tots did not take a nap.

3. We will not go to Sea World during the rainy season.

4. You should not go before noon.

5. The bird would not fly near me.

6. The corn was not in the barn.

7. The children may not play outside the house during the storm.

8. You must not drive through the tunnel without bright headlights.

Reminder: In the word CANNOT, underline only the CAN.

9. I cannot understand your answer.

10. Without food, your body cannot function.

Reminder: If NOT appears N'T, do not underline the N'T.

11. Some cars haven't been sold at the auction.

12. The doctor didn't write a prescription for her patient.

13. Shouldn't the officers leave after the program?

14. From my point of view, you don't deserve a prize for that.

15. I won't go without you.

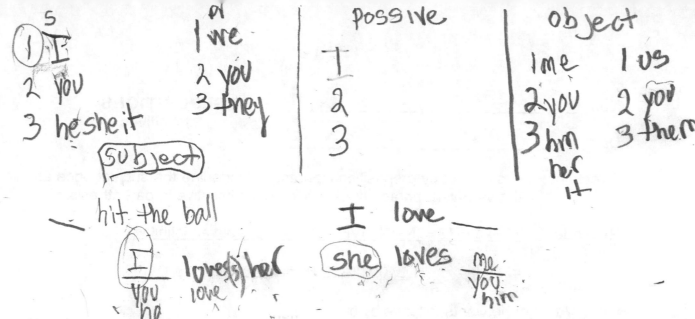

Sometimes *to* will come before a verb. <u>TO + VERB is an infinitive;</u> TO + VERB IS NOT A PREPOSITIONAL PHRASE.

To dance, *to sing*, *to yell*, *to be*, *to leave*, *to go* are examples of infinitives. Do NOT cross them out as prepositional phrases. Place an infinitive in parenthesis.

Example: I like (to sing) ~~in the morning~~.

       A. in the morning   -   a prepositional phrase

       B. to sing   - infinitive   (to + verb)

Date_____

Directions: Cross out any prepositional phrases. Underline the subject once and the verb/verb phrase twice. Place each infinitive in parenthesis.

Reminder: TO + VERB = INFINITIVE. Do not cross out an infinitive.

   Example: I like (to go) to the movies.

1.   At night he wants to leave by bus.

2.   The child decided to run to the baseball game.

3.   After dinner the guests desire to enjoy some coffee.

4.   The artist likes to paint during the morning.

5.   The teams wanted to practice after school.

6.   She forgot to look for her lost watch.

7.   The rider hopes to be in the rodeo.

8.   For an hour the customers waited for dinner.

9.   His uncle pretended to twist his arm.

10.   They like to play against that team.

11.   The diplomat waited to hear the end of the speech.

12.   The cheerleader ran to catch the bus for the game.

13.   Before the game the spectators rose to sing the national anthem.

14.   During the parade the marcher stopped to rest for a moment.

15.   A few of the guests at the wedding wanted to dance with the bride.

In an imperative sentence, the subject is (<u>You</u>).

    I. An imperative sentence gives a command.

   II. (<u>You</u>) is termed **YOU UNDERSTOOD**.   It is written at the beginning of the sentence, underlined, and placed in parenthesis.

EXAMPLES:

    A. Go down the street.

       (<u>You</u>) <u>Go</u> down the street.

    B. Please look at me.

       (<u>You</u>) Please <u>look</u> at me.

    C. Put the scissors in the drawer.

       (<u>You</u>) <u>Put</u> the scissors in the drawer.

Directions: Cross out any prepositional phrases. Underline the subject once and the verb/verb phrase twice.

Reminder: In an imperative sentence (command), the subject is often (You).

1.   Put the packages from my grandparents on the kitchen table.

2.   During the thunderstorm, light the candles.

3.   Tell the class about your summer.

4.   Sit between Tracy and my brother during the game.

5.   Jump on the wagon.

6.   Look under the sink for the paper bag.

7.   After class give the teacher your paper.

8.   Walk toward me.

9.   From the town square, drive three miles to the inn.

10.   Stop in the middle of the road.

11.   Pay for the tour inside the museum.

12.   Hurry down the hall for your next meeting.

13.   Near the end of the year, take a trip to Paris.

14.   Go into the apartment for an umbrella.

15.   In January send the children to the nurse for a hearing test.

Name_____ **PREPOSITIONS**

Date_____

Directions: Cross out any prepositional phrases. Underline the subject once
and the verb/verb phrase twice.

1. John walked along the trail during the summer.

2. In one cage we saw a huge bird from the jungles of Brazil.

3. A rose bush with sharp thorns grew inside our fence.

4. She divided the candy among the children at the party.

5. The boys will go across the street, through the alley, and into the park.

6. Beyond that hill is a house without a roof.

7. Near that city and past a mountain is a pot of gold for you.

8. Along the muddy road and against the rain, the lady walked underneath an
umbrella.

9. Above the third shelf, you will find books about Abe Lincoln and concerning
other aspects of American history.

10. In the middle of the party, the lady dashed out the door without her coat.

11. Beneath the tree slumbered an old man with his dog.

12. The lad darted beyond his mother's reach during the game.

13. Walk past the gate and through the door to find a beautiful room without
furniture.

14. The dessert was stored in the refrigerator until the end of the meal.

15. Behind me sat a clown with his balloons and lollipops.

Directions: Cross out any prepositional phrases. Underline the subject once and the verb/verb phrase twice.

1.   The bird flew in and out among the branches of the oak tree.

2.   She looked up in the sky.

3.   Do you live near to me?

4.   The tourists went down into the caverns.

5.   The model strolled in and looked around the room.

6.   The child dashed over to the edge of the canyon.

7.   During the hayride, the leader jumped off of the wagon.

8.   Someone like Jane may come over for a visit.

9.   In the breeze, the flower swayed up and down.

10.   Dad will come along on the picnic tomorrow.

11.   Our family went outside to take a picture.

12.   Go in through the side entrance.

13.   He crawled below the deck and remained inside.

14.   The secretary and the accountant walked around and found the missing notebook in the trash can.

15.   The oven has been turned off for an hour and thirty minutes.

I. Words that end in ly are usually adverbs. They are not prepositions.

  Examples: A. We went into the pool carefully.

              ADV.
      We went ~~into the pool~~ carefully.

      B. Slowly the banker walked into the vault.

      ADV.
      Slowly the banker walked ~~into the vault~~.

II. If you are not sure if a word is part of the verb, try putting TO in front of the word. If you cannot divide it into present (today), and past (yesterday) tenses, the word probably is not a verb.

  Examples: A. The pie was good.

      Can you say "To Good"? Today I good; yesterday I gooded.
      Good does not make sense here, and thus good is not part
      of the verb.

      The pie was good.

      B. Marty was happy.

      Can you say "To Happy"? Today I happy; yesterday I
      happied. Happy does not make sense here, and thus,
      happy is not part of the verb.

      Marty was happy.

Name_____

Date_____

Directions: Cross out any prepositional phrases. Underline the subject once and
the verb/verb phrase twice.

1.   In the bushes along the road stood an elephant with purple spots in front of his
eyes.

2.   You may go at noon except Saturdays.

3.   Until Christmas, the shoppers will travel through stores, across streets, between
cars in parking lots, and past decorated windows in search of the perfect gift.

4.   At the beginning of the year, students must learn rules concerning the
playground and regarding the lunch line.

5.   On the fifth of November, everyone but my brother and sister should arrive in
Phoenix by plane.

6.   During the football game, many spectators sat behind the goal posts and went
frequently to the snack bar.

7.   Near the museum stands a statue of Paul Bunyan and his ox.

8.   Go down the street for a cup of milk.

9.   You may not go between the buildings or outside the school campus from eight
o'clock until four o'clock.

10.   The can of soup is below the sink, above the stove, or beside the refrigerator.

11.   Over the bridge, under the freeway, and through the field ran the team.

12.   After the game, the girls in the blue sweaters walked to the auditorium.

13.   After class you must go out the door and into the street for a parade.

14.   The book concerning politics is against discrimination.

15.   By noon we had walked over a mile beyond our goal.

Directions: Cross out any prepositional phrases. Underline the subject once
and the verb/verb phrase twice.

1.   Over that hill and past the bridge jogged a lady with her new dog.

2.   Throughout the night the security guard walked from store to store.

3.   The meeting concerning the new town hall met at the library.

4.   During the celebration everyone except Mother flew to San Diego.

5.   On the moonlit night, the deer appeared in a field by the quiet stream.

6.   The student walked out the door among his friends during graduation practice.

7.   The treasure was buried underneath a tree near the railroad car.

8.   The movie star walked among the fans and across the street to the theater.

9.   Out the door and into the car scurried the woman with her brown briefcase.

10.   During the carnival, the small child squirmed out of the reach of his parents.

11.   The person beside me plays a flute in our band.

12.   The dancers waltzed off the floor and went outside for some cool air.

13.   Go to the snack bar before the movie.

14.   The swimmer dived off the board and swam toward me.

15.   From 5 o'clock until 8 o'clock, I wandered around the building to find my mother.

Name_____

Date_____

Directions: Cross out any prepositional phrases. Underline the subject once
              and the verb/verb phrase twice.

1.   Some spectators in the back row of the rodeo jeered at the clowns after the last
     event.

2.   Around the house and across the street ran a little squirrel with an acorn in his
     mouth.

3.   During the storm, the wind blew inside the house from the north.

4.   Our maid cleaned the top of the counter and looked amid the groceries
     throughout the refrigerator.

5.   We will be at the mall by Sears within an hour.

6.   Three of the students were against shorter vacations for teachers.

7.   The letters for Mary and John concerning college and regarding admission
     costs were outside the house in the mailbox.

8.   All cars except the blue one were sold before noon by that salesman.

9.   Between you and me, the crickets were singing in the oleander after the rain.

10. Our plane flew through a storm over the Rio Grande River.

11. The yacht sailed across the Potomac River and under the Mason Bridge.

12. Do not go past the line until the end of the game.

13. All of my cousins except John went to the zoo without their jackets.

14. Down the slopes toward the Swiss village came the mountain climbers.

15. The matter concerning the parking ticket was decided by the judge at the court
     on Monday.

Directions: Cross out any prepositional phrases. Underline the subject once and
the verb/verb phrase twice.

1.   In the early morning, the birds chirped in the back of the house near the pond.

2.   After this year, the students must go to the lakes for a short vacation.

3.   We walked through the forest, past the old mill, and between two highways.

4.   Place the boxes over the sink or under the cupboard.

5.   Without your help, I would lose at chess and checkers.

6.   The man threw his fishing pole to his friend across the stream.

7.   Many of the cows were lying in the field after the storm.

8.   Behind the woods and over that hill, you will find a prize in a pile of rubble.

9.   Look across the street and down the road before crossing.

10.   From the looks of the weather, the children should not go outside the house.

11.   Before the meeting, the group talked about women's liberation.

12.   Up above the rooftops is a beautiful full moon with a haze around it.

13.   Don't tell anyone about the decision concerning the talent show and the puppet
production.

14.   Atop the fence at the edge of the town sat a hobo throughout the hot day in July.

15.   Before recess, groups of students were not allowed to go out into the hallway
without the teacher.

Directions: Cross out any prepositional phrases. Underline the subject once
and the verb/verb phrase twice.

1.   After the session with the band leader, the team didn't want to go without you.

2.   Within the hour, the mail person delivered a box for Mrs. Hill.

3.   Archaeologists with dedication dig for days in search of artifacts.

4.   Beyond the wall there is a lovely puppy from your dad.

5.   Around the turn in the road and about two miles down the road, there is located
an old inn.

6.   During the American Revolution, Paine wrote a book concerning liberty and
justice.

7.   Johnathon lives near to you, past that old bridge, and under an oak tree.

8.   Find the marbles under the sink, beneath the first shelf, below the bathroom
vanity, or underneath a rock in the front yard.

9.   Over the bridge, past the toll booth, and through the tunnel, the cars of New York
travel.

10.   His statement regarding our defense was good.

11.   In the middle of the mutiny, Columbus's men saw birds and knew about land.

12.   He went up in the elevator and out onto the observation deck.

13.   Give the message about her illness to your mother today after school.

14.   A few of the games were played during the evening hours before dark.

15.   Did any of the mothers fill in the forms about the children's health records?

Name_____   **PREPOSITIONS**

Date_____

Directions: Cross out any prepositional phrases. Underline the subject once and
the verb/verb phrase twice.

1. After the game, the team ate at Sambo's Restaurant on the freeway.

2. During the class, a student pitched a book out the window.

3. The girl stumbled over a rock and was taken to emergency.

4. The ladies and men of the photography club met at the library at seven o'clock
in the evening.

5. In October, the teacher gave a test about fractions.

6. Through the forest and past the old mill lives a carpenter with his horse and
dog.

7. In July, school is not in session.

8. Come into the house and take off your shoes in the kitchen.

9. During the spring break, the members of our club visited Maine.

10. Quietly and carefully remove the boxes from the premises.

11. The meal of meat loaf, au gratin potatoes, and beans was good.

12. The lid of the tea kettle was closed.

13. After the sale, every woman went into the store, down the escalator, and to the
bargains in the basement.

14. The picture of Martha Washington hung in the closet by the fireplace.

15. The walls of the mansion were of gold and marble.

**PREPOSITION
REVIEW**

A. Infinitives:

Directions: Cross out any prepositional phrases. Underline the subject once and the verb/verb phrase twice. Place any infinitive in parenthesis ( ).

1. Marnie's mother and father want to go to New York during the summer.

2. A group of parents went into the auditorium to hear several speakers.

3. They like to eat lunch at that cafe on Brock Street.

4. The reporter decided to interview the mayor of our town.

5. His sister pretended to be angry with him.

6. Their car did not need to remain in the repair shop for a long time.

7. Many tourists stopped to read brochures about Pearl Harbor.

B. Verb Phrases:

Directions: Cross out any prepositional phrases. Underline the subject once and the verb/verb phrase twice.

1. The garbage truck has stopped near the corner of Washington Street.

2. May I sit between Todd and you for ten minutes?

3. Everyone but John must have taken his bathing suit with him.

4. We will be rowing on the lake after sunset today.

5. Does the policeman attend the church beside the new park?

6. Your name should not have been written in cursive.

7. Mark's friend cannot come until the end of the winter.

C. **Imperative Sentences:**

Directions: Cross out any prepositional phrases. Underline the subject once and the verb/verb phrase twice.

1. Give this tip to the waiter in the checkered shirt.

2. Remove your shoes at the door, please.

3. Near the end of the day, please take a bath.

4. Follow the interstate highway through the tunnels.

5. Drive to the side of the road immediately.

6. After the meeting, hand a pamphlet to everyone but Mr. Barton.

7. Sit across the table from me during the luncheon with those guests.

D. **Compound Objects:**

Directions: Cross out any prepositional phrases.   Underline the subject once and the verb/verb phrase twice.

1. Mrs. Little stepped into the rain without a hat or an umbrella.

2. A young lady with red hair sat between Mary and me.

3. A package from Grandma and Grandpa was delivered before lunch.

4. In July, August, or September, their family will visit Montana.

5. Flowers grow along the walk and driveway of the new home.

6. One of the houses by the sea won't be completed until fall or winter.

7. Go past the library and police station to reach the courthouse.

E. **Compound Subjects:**

Directions: Cross out any prepositional phrases. Underline the subject once
and the verb/verb phrase twice.

1.   Doug and his new bride vacationed in Florida.

2.   During the fair, a country singer and his band performed for a huge crowd.

3.   A bowl of various fruits and a plate of cheeses are beside the crackers.

4.   Underneath the steps of a small cottage lay a tawny cat and a black dog.

5.   Ted's brother and friend chased around the park on roller blades.

6.   Some businesswomen and politicians are meeting to discuss the economy.

7.   The attorneys and the judge went into the chambers for a private discussion.

F. **Compound Verbs:**

Directions: Cross out any prepositional phrases.   Underline the subject once
and the verb/verb phrase twice.

1.   The instructor stood among the students and chatted with them.

2.   Did the technician fix the television or tell Kurt to buy another?

3.   Some children walked along the road and picked flowers.

4.   After supper, we cleared the table and rinsed our dishes.

5.   Go inside the shed and get sponges and a pail for water, please.

6.   My glass duck from Aunt Betty has fallen on the stairs and has broken into many
pieces.

7.   Everyone but Jonah stood and cheered for the contestants.

G. Preposition or Adverb:

Directions: Cross out any prepositional phrases.   Underline the subject once and the verb/verb phrase twice. Label any adverb-Adv.

1. That small child often falls down on his roller skates.

2. Lenny's brothers are playing outside in the rain.

3. The dog went outside and ran around in a circle.

4. Please look up toward the skylight in the ceiling.

5. The teenagers walked in and out among the fair booths.

6. Are Annie and James lagging behind again?

7. One of the players on the other team came over to talk to my brother.

8. We walked inside and looked for a guide.

9. Rob will come along with us.

10. Several girls rode by on their bikes and waved.

11. A frightened child would not come near.

12. You may not go through without a ticket.

13. Please come by in the morning.

14. The mother walked inside and checked the cake in the oven.

15. She approached the table, looked underneath, and found a giggling toddler.

16. The shopper looked both ways at the intersection and hurried across.

Name_____

Date_____

Directions: Cross out any prepositional phrases. Underline the subject once
             and the verb/verb phrase twice.

1.   From June until the end of August, Carl lives in Alabama.

2.   Some boys and girls rode their bikes along a path.

3.   The man walked behind a car and across the street.

4.   The laughing girls jumped into the stream and chased each other through the
     water.

5.   Finish your project by the end of the week.

6.   Everyone except the the senator attended the meeting concerning the proposed
     tax increase.

7.   During the wedding reception, the bride sat near the groom and her attendants.

8.   Within a week, the detective had checked with several witnesses.

9.   Her dog likes to lie upon a pillow throughout the afternoon.

10.   One of his cats will not go outside after a rainstorm.

11.   For several minutes, several toddlers danced around in a circle.

12.   At five o'clock on June 1st, my aunt will be baptized by her minister.

13.   The discussion between Lori and her mother was regarding their weekend
      plans.

14.   One house beside the museum has been deserted since last February.

15.   That rancher walked out beyond his corral and stared toward the woods.

Name_____

Date_____

Directions: Cross out any prepositional phrases.   Underline the subject once
and the verb/verb phrase twice.

1.   Without hesitation, the rabbit hopped underneath some brush.

2.   Dad looked above the stove for a fire extinguisher.

3.   The readers searched among the shelves for books about frogs and toads.

4.   Clean the glass under the coffee table with this sponge.

5.   Before the parade, everyone walked toward the town square.

6.   The company has displayed all of its products but the new cleanser.

7.   Your jacket has fallen down behind the green flowered sofa.

8.   Place these washcloths and towels in the cupboard beneath the sink.

9.   Their grandparents from Colorado stay inside during the winter.

10.   Yesterday, the skater fell down and rolled off the low curb .

11.   Miss Jones and her friend walk past the park on their way to the gym.

12.   The athlete jumped over a hurdle and darted for the finish line.

13.   Insects like grasshoppers, centipedes, and dragonflies don't scare them.

14.   At the beginning of the class, Mrs. Harmon talked about the Middle East.

15.   The chimney sweep laid his tools against the fireplace and peered up the
chimney.

DIRECT OBJECTS

Direct objects receive the action of the verb. In order to have a direct object, there must be an "action" verb in the sentence. Although occasionally a prepositional phrase may serve as a direct object, it occurs so seldom that, once again, students are instructed to cross out prepositional phrases and not label those as direct objects.

DIRECT OBJECT:

A. I kicked the desk. (What received the action? <u>Desk</u>)

B. I pulled Jane's hair. (What received the action? <u>Hair</u>)

C. I tossed the pencil. (What received the action? <u>Pencil</u>)

D. Sally hit the ball ~~into left field~~. (What received the action? <u>Ball</u>)

Name_____

Date_____

Directions: Cross out any prepositional phrases. Underline the subject once and
the verb/verb phrase twice. Label direct object(s)-D.O.

1.   The child grabbed the toy from his brother.

2.   Susan chose the pink dress for the dance.

3.   After dinner Father washed the dishes.

4.   We ate bananas for breakfast.

5.   The girl hit the ball to left field.

6.   The cook fried an egg in that frying pan.

7.   During the ceremony, the speaker presented an award to the student.

8.   The other school played a game against our school.

9.   The plumber took her tools with her.

10.   The gardener chased the rabbits off his property.

11.   The baby threw the rattle onto the floor.

12.   The officer parked the car near the police station.

13.   At that restaurant the waiters carry large trays.

14.   The hikers carried their packs across town.

15.   Set the groceries by the microwave oven.

Direct Objects

A sentence may contain compound direct objects. This means that there are two or more direct objects within a sentence.

Examples:

    A. The toddler chased the dog and cat around the house.

                               D.O.   D.O.

The <u>toddler</u> <u>chased</u> the dog and cat ~~around the house~~.

    B. The artist drew birds, flowers, and butterflies in the painting.

                        D.O.   D.O.   D.O.

The <u>artist</u> <u>drew</u> birds, flowers, and butterflies ~~in the painting~~.

Directions: Cross out any prepositional phrases. Underline the subject once and
the verb/verb phrase twice. Label the direct object(s)-D.O.

1.   We ate bacon and eggs for breakfast.

2.   The traveler dropped his luggage and his keys beside me.

3.   Within an hour, the detective had caught the burglar and his accomplice.

4.   During the sale, my mother purchased a new blouse and some earrings.

5.   John and Dave baked cookies and coconut pie for the bake sale.

6.   The farmer planted tomatoes and peppers in his garden.

7.   Take fried chicken and potato salad on the picnic.

8.   Before his trip, the pilot ironed his pants and shirt.

9.   You will find the mop or broom in the laundry room.

10.   Are you buying French fries and a coke at our favorite restaurant?

11.   Some of the students took their books and notebooks with them.

12.   The shopper selected fish and broccoli for dinner.

13.   A couple received a toaster and a blender for a wedding gift.

14.   I placed toys and other junk under my bed.

15.   Over the door we hung ribbons and balloons for the birthday party.

VERBS

The verb of a sentence expresses an action or simply states a fact.

Examples: Jenny <u>cut</u> down the old oak tree.   (action)

Waiters <u>set</u> the table for the buffet.   (action)

Our senator <u>is</u> happy about the new law.   (fact)

My brother <u>was</u> in a bad mood.   (fact)

Verbs that simply state a fact are often called **<u>state of being verbs</u>**.

VERBS

There are two main types of verbs: **action and linking**. Action verbs do exactly what the term implies. Action verbs show action. You will note that in order to have a direct object, the sentence must contain an action verb.

Linking verbs are difficult. First, they do not show action. They do exactly what their name implies. They link two parts in the sentence. They link the subject with either a noun or pronoun (called a predicate nominative) or with an adjective (called a predicate adjective).

State of being verbs simply help to make a statement. The most commonly used state of being verbs come from the infinitive *to be*.

CONTRACTIONS

To contract means to draw together. Thus, in forming contractions, we draw together two words to make one word. We do this by dropping some letter or letters and inserting an apostrophe (') where the letter(s) is(are) missing.

Suggestions:

A. Make sure that your apostrophe looks like an apostrophe and not a chicken scratch mark.

B. Place the apostrophe exactly where the letter(s) are missing.

C. The contraction should be written in broken form so that mistakes are avoided.

This *don't*   Not This *don't*

Contractions =	verb	+	word		Contractions =	word	+	verb
don't	do	+	not		I'm	I	+	am
doesn't	does	+	not		I've	I	+	have
didn't	did	+	not		I'd	I	+	would
hasn't	has	+	not		I'll	I	+	will
haven't	have	+	not		you'll	you	+	will
hadn't	had	+	not		they'll	they	+	will
isn't	is	+	not		we'll	we	+	will
aren't	are	+	not		he's	he	+	is
wasn't	was	+	not		he'd	he	+	would
weren't	were	+	not		she's	she	+	is
mustn't	must	+	not		they've	they	+	have
mightn't	might	+	not		they're	they	+	are
shouldn't	should	+	not		it's	it	+	is
couldn't	could	+	not		who's	who	+	is
wouldn't	would	+	not		what's	what	+	is
won't	will	+	not		where's	where	+	is
can't	can	+	not		here's	here	+	is
					there's	there	+	is

Directions: Write the contraction in the space provided.

Example: ___What's___   <u>What is</u> your name?

1. _____   <u>Here is</u> your order.

2. _____   The emergency kit <u>will not</u> fit into the glove compartment of his car.

3. _____   The guests <u>could not</u> finish their dessert.

4. _____   <u>I have</u> so much to accomplish.

5. _____   The macrame <u>was not</u> completed until last weekend.

6. _____   I think that <u>he would</u> be happier in a warmer climate.

7. _____   <u>We will</u> take the chair lift to the mountain slope.

8. _____   The shipment of cameras <u>has not</u> arrived.

9. _____   <u>They are</u> finished with their latest report.

10. _____   Our antique china closet <u>is not</u> refinished.

11. _____   <u>You will</u> want a green rug for the living room.

12. _____   This blanket <u>cannot</u> be washed.

13. _____   <u>What is</u> the name of your new friend?

14. _____   Some of your test answers <u>do not</u> make sense.

15. _____   Our saw <u>would not</u> cut into that piece of hard wood.

Name_____

Date_____

Directions: Write the contraction in the space provided.

Example: ____How's____   How is your father?

1. _____   Do not go fishing without me.

2. _____   I told him that I will be there at four o'clock.

3. _____   Where is the Alamo?

4. _____   Some of the sheep are not being herded by the dog.

5. _____   She is a very capable woodcarver.

6. _____   The blue house did not get painted this summer.

7. _____   They have just returned from a trip to China.

8. _____   Do you think it is acceptable to send flowers to a young man?

9. _____   There is no milk for my cereal.

10. _____   Fortunately many of the artifacts had not broken.

11. _____   I was not informed of the problem.

12. _____   Our leader explained that I will give the speech at the next assembly.

13. _____   If you should not choose to go, Mary will take your place.

14. _____   Here is your missing assignment.

15. _____   Have you met the person who is director of our recreation club?

42

LIST OF HELPING (AUXILIARY) VERBS

DO	HAS	IS	MAY
DOES	HAVE	AM	MUST
DID	HAD	ARE	MIGHT
		WAS	SHOULD
		WERE	COULD
		BE	WOULD
		BEING	SHALL
		BEEN	WILL
			CAN

VERB PHRASES

Sometimes two or more words make up a verb. This is called a verb phrase.

The last word in a verb phrase is called the **main verb**; other words are called

auxiliary (helping) verbs.

Verb Phrase	=	helping verb(s)	+	main verb
should go	=	should	+	go
has been given	=	has been	+	given
will be leaving	=	will be	+	leaving

In a declarative (statement) sentence, the verb phrase is usually together.

    Example: That window <u>must have been broken</u> by a rock.

        must have been + broken

In an interrogative (question) sentence, the verb phrase is often split.

    Example: <u>Have</u> my jeans <u>been washed</u> yet?

        Have been + washed

VERBS
Verb Phrases

Directions: Cross out any prepositional phrases. Underline the subject once and
the verb/verb phrase twice. Place the auxiliary (helping) verb(s) and
the main verb of each sentence on the line indicated.

Example: The <u>car</u> <u>will</u> not <u>start</u>!   __will__   __start__

HELPING VERB(S)   MAIN VERB

1.   Will you answer the phone?   _____   _____

2.   Dr. Jones must have shown your sister the
x-rays.   _____   _____

3.   May Connie and I leave now?   _____   _____

4.   There must have been an accident on this
corner.   _____   _____

5.   Did Katy return her imperfect briefcase?   _____   _____

6.   Was any chair sold for fifty dollars?   _____   _____

7.   Peter should not have stayed at the park.   _____   _____

8.   My student has had strep throat three times
this year.   _____   _____

9.   Doesn't your dad cook breakfast every
Saturday morning?   _____   _____

10.   They could fix the light after working hours.   _____   _____

11.   I'm searching for the word in the dictionary.   _____   _____

12.   Has anyone seen the Egyptian pyramids?   _____   _____

13.   The jury might decide the verdict today.   _____   _____

14.   I shall inform you of my decision.   _____   _____

15.   That would never have occurred to me.   _____   _____

Name_____   **VERBS**
                                          Verb Phrases
Date_____

Directions: Cross out any prepositional phrases. Underline the subject once and the
               verb/verb phrase twice. Place the auxiliary (helping) verb(s) and the
               main verb of each sentence on the line provided.
               Example: We <u>have gone</u> often.   ___have___   ___gone___

		HELPING VERBS	MAIN VERB

1.   These apples must have been grown in
      Pennsylvania.   _____ _____

2.   Sissy will not be attending her class reunion. _____ _____

3.   Were the investors planning a convention
      in Lake Tahoe?   _____ _____

4.   I might have lost my new tennis racket. _____ _____

5.   Which of the fabrics do you like?   _____ _____

6.   Whose car has been parked at the bottom
      of the hill?   _____ _____

7.   Those plants should be watered daily. _____ _____

8.   Have you been in the Sears Tower
      in Chicago?   _____ _____

9.   The jeweler would not remove the diamond
      necklace from the window display.   _____ _____

10.   Who will be coming to the graduation dance? _____ _____

11.   The photographer has taken a family portrait. _____ _____

12.   Am I expected at the Brown's home for dinner?_____ _____

13.   You are wearing my favorite color.   _____ _____

14.   By dusk, we will have been in this car for five
      hours.   _____ _____

15.   Shall I ask my parents for their approval? _____ _____
46

VERBS

In regular verbs, the past and the past participle are the same. The past tense is formed by adding _ed_ to the verb (bark-barked).

Examples:

Infinitive	Present	Past	Past Participle
to walk	walk(s)	walked	(had) walked
to jump	jump(s)	jumped	(had) jumped
to grab	grab(s)	grabbed	(had) grabbed
to boast	boast(s)	boasted	(had) boasted

IRREGULAR VERBS

Irregular verbs do not add <u>ed</u> to the past tense (fall-fell). Usually the past tense and the past participle form are not the same (spoke-spoken).

Examples:

Infinitive	Present	Past	Past Participle
to run	run(s)	ran	(had) run
to know	know(s)	knew	(had) known
to bring	bring(s)	brought	(had) brought*

*You will note that the past and the past participle forms of <u>to bring</u> are the same. However, <u>to bring</u> qualifies as an irregular verb because <u>ed</u> is not added to form the past tense.

IRREGULAR VERBS

Infinitive	Present	Past	Present Participle	Past Participle*
To be	is, am, are	was, were	being	been
To beat	beat(s)	beat	beating	beaten
To begin	begin(s)	began	beginning	begun
To blow	blow(s)	blew	blowing	blown
To break	break(s)	broke	breaking	broken
To bring	bring(s)	brought	bringing	brought
To burst	burst(s)	burst	bursting	burst
To buy	buy(s)	bought	buying	bought
To choose	choose(s)	chose	choosing	chosen
To come	come(s)	came	coming	come
To do	do, does	did	doing	done
To drink	drink(s)	drank	drinking	drunk
To drive	drive(s)	drove	driving	driven
To eat	eat(s)	ate	eating	eaten
To fall	fall(s)	fell	falling	fallen
To fly	fly, flies	flew	flying	flown
To freeze	freeze(s)	froze	freezing	frozen
To give	give(s)	gave	giving	given
To go	go, goes	went	going	gone
To grow	grow(s)	grew	growing	grown
To have	have, has	had	having	had
To hang	hang(s)	hanged, hung	hanging	hanged, hung
To know	know(s)	knew	knowing	known
To lay	lay(s)	laid	laying	laid
To leave	leave(s)	left	leaving	left

*Uses a helping verb such as <u>has</u>, <u>have</u>, or <u>had</u>.

IRREGULAR VERBS

Infinitive	Present	Past	Present Participle	Past Participle*
To lie	lie(s)	lay	lying	lain
To ride	ride(s)	rode	riding	ridden
To ring	ring(s)	rang	ringing	rung
To rise	rise(s)	rose	rising	risen
To run	run(s)	ran	running	run
To see	see(s)	saw	seeing	seen
To set	set(s)	set	setting	set
To shake	shake(s)	shook	shaking	shaken
To shrink	shrink(s)	shrank	shrinking	shrunk
To sing	sing(s)	sang	singing	sung
To sink	sink(s)	sank	sinking	sunk
To sit	sit(s)	sat	sitting	sat
To speak	speak(s)	spoke	speaking	spoken
To spring	spring(s)	sprang	springing	sprung
To steal	steal(s)	stole	stealing	stolen
To swim	swim(s)	swam	swimming	swum
To swear	swear(s)	swore	swearing	sworn
To take	take(s)	took	taking	taken
To teach	teach(es)	taught	teaching	taught
To throw	throw(s)	threw	throwing	thrown
To wear	wear(s)	wore	wearing	worn
To write	write(s)	wrote	writing	written

*The past participle form is the form of the verb used with <u>have</u>, <u>has</u>, or <u>had</u>.

Name_____ **VERB FORMS**

Date_____

Directions: Place the correct verb form(s) in the space provided.

INFINITIVE	PRESENT	PAST	PAST PARTICIPLE

Name_____   **VERB FORMS**

Date_____

Directions: Place the correct verb form(s) in the space provided.

INFINITIVE   PRESENT   PAST   PAST PARTICIPLE

_____

_____

_____

_____

_____

_____

_____

_____

_____

_____

_____

_____

_____

_____

_____

_____

_____

_____

_____

_____

_____

Name_____

Date_____

Directions: Cross out any prepositional phrases. Underline the subject once
and the verb/verb phrase twice.

Example: I should have (chose, chosen) a newer car.

1.   The flag had (flew, flown) at half mast.

2.   We have (choose, chosen) a new sofa.

3.   The pupil had not (brang, brought) the homework.

4.   Has the lamp been (broke, broken)?

5.   The graduate was (gave, given) a gift.

6.   Has the choir ever (sung, sang) that tune?

7.   We could have (run, ran) another mile.

8.   Our family had (drove, driven) to Arcadia National Park.

9.   The seamstress should have (boughten, bought) more fabric.

10.   By the end of the contest, the contestants will have (ate, eaten) at least two
pies.

11.   I could have (drank, drunk) a gallon of water.

12.   Their bus must have already (came, come).

13.   Has your blouse (shrank, shrunk) in the laundry?

14.   Jordy could have (wore, worn) your costume to the party.

15.   Has the sun (rose, risen) earlier than usual?

Name_____

Date_____

Directions: Cross out any prepositional phrases. Underline the subject once
              and the verb/verb phrase twice.

      Example: The <u>speaker</u> <u>has</u> (<u>come,</u> came) early.

1.   Our balloons have (burst, bursted).

2.   Has the president (shook, shaken) your hand?

3.   The laundry had been (hang, hung) on the clothesline.

4.   That ship must have (sank, sunk) during the battle.

5.   They have (stole, stolen) that idea from another company.

6.   The boxer (sprang, sprung) to his feet during the count.

7.   I may have (did, done) the problem incorrectly.

8.   Ice cubes were (froze, frozen) in pretty trays.

9.   My opponent has (beat, beaten) me at the game of chess.

10.   She (began, begun) to feel ill.

11.   Wind may have (blew, blown) the table over.

12.   Has the puppy (laid, lain) there long?

13.   He must have (saw, seen) me at the dance.

14.   A rock was (threw, thrown) through the large window.

15.   Several children (swam, swum) in the lake.

Directions: Cross out any prepositional phrases. Underline the subject once
and the verb/verb phrase twice.

Example: He has (gave, underline{given}) me his old hat.

1.   In July our neighbors had (went, gone) to Europe.

2.   Have you (rode, ridden) the gray mare?

3.   A mountain climber must have (ran, run) into difficulty.

4.   Has Grandma (knew, known) your parents for a long time?

5.   George should not have (wrote, written) the note.

6.   The naughty child (sank, sunk) down into the seat.

7.   A witness was (swore, sworn) in by the judge.

8.   Records were (broke, broken) during the Olympics.

9.   You should have (chose, chosen) something more practical.

10.   Had he (ate, eaten) before surgery?

11.   The soloist (sung, sang) very loudly.

12.   The real estate agent must have (brung, brought) thirty people through our
home.

13.   Some of my classmates (done, did) their homework at school.

14.   Our brother would not have (drunk, drank) milk with each meal.

15.   Jason should have (went, gone) earlier.

Name_____   **IRREGULAR VERBS**

Date_____

Directions: Cross out any prepositional phrases. Underline the subject once
              and the verb phrase twice.

     Example: The <u>balloon</u> <u>should</u> not <u>have</u> (bursted, <u>burst</u>) so easily.

1.   The bestseller should have been (given, gave) to my mother.

2.   Hot dogs were (chose, chosen) for the lunch menu.

3.   The mail must have (came, come) early.

4.   He might have (gone, went) to the symphony after dinner.

5.   Has the road map (fallen, fell) on the floor of the car?

6.   During the early hours, the repairman (done, did) his tasks.

7.   The papers on the sofa have (lain, lay) there all day.

8.   By December the business lady will have (flew, flown) 50,000 miles.

9.   Has a copy of this test been (ran, run)?

10. You should have (saw, seen) the look on his face.

11. A florist had (spoke, spoken) about flower arrangements at our gardening
     meeting.

12. I (seen, saw) Joe at the basketball game.

13. The clothes were (shaken, shook) after removal from the dryer.

14. Was the accident victim (took, taken) to a local hospital?

15. The sweepstakes winner has (written, wrote) a clever jingle.

56

Directions: Cross out any prepositional phrases. Underline the subject once
              and the verb/verb phrase twice. Label direct object(s)-D.O.

1.   I put the casserole into the oven.

2.   The campers made a fire at night.

3.   We cleaned the pool after the dust storm.

4.   Before dawn, the farmer milked the cows.

5.   During the emergency, the lifeguard pulled the child from the water.

6.   Mary chased Susan and her friend around the room.

7.   Santa left the gifts under the tree.

8.   A traveler caught a taxi to the bus terminal.

9.   Within two minutes the monkey had eaten three bananas.

10.   A handyman placed paneling on the wall in our den.

11.   Several of the squirrels had hidden nuts in the tree.

12.   At noon we should have eaten more pizza.

13.   Has John or Grace taken the test today?

14.   Roofers placed new shingles on the house.

15.   Take this envelope and that package to the post office.

Directions: Cross out any prepositional phrases. Underline the subject once and the verb/verb phrase twice. Label the direct object(s)-D.O.

1.   The coach carried the injured player off the field.

2.   At the soda fountain each of us ate a sundae.

3.   Have you seen my watch anywhere?

4.   Birds ate the seeds in our garden.

5.   They bought a new tape for their collection.

6.   Dr. Abernathy gave sugarless lollipops to his young patients.

7.   Have you dialed the phone?

8.   I cannot bring my whistle or horn to your house.

9.   The ladies' club served coffee and tea at the end of the meeting.

10.   We will not cut the grass until evening.

11.   Give your book to the new student.

12.   The housekeeper washed the floors and dusted the furniture.

13.   Did you send me a card on my birthday?

14.   Someone hid my keys under the table and scribbled the walls with purple and green crayons.

15.   Is the milkman delivering milk in your neighborhood?

SIT/SET

<u>To sit</u>:   means to rest
<u>To set</u>:   means to place or to put

FORMS:

Infinitive	Present	Past	Present Participle	Past Participle
To sit	sit(s)	sat	sitting	(had) sat
To set	set(s)	set	setting	(had) set

Two basic items for sit/set:

A. Both *sit* and *set* are irregular verbs and must be learned.

B. *Set* requires a direct object.*

Examples:

He is (sitting, setting) on the porch.

He <u>is</u> (<u>sitting,</u> setting) on the porch.   (There is no direct object in the sentence. Thus, *sitting* is used. In addition, *resting* can be inserted for *sitting*.)

The librarian (sit, set) the books down.

The librarian (sit, <u>set</u>) the books down. (Because *books* is the direct object, the answer has to be *set*. In addition, *put* can be inserted for *set*.)

Unfortunately, there are times when *to set* will NOT have a direct object. Give full attention to the meaning of *place* or *put*. If *placed* can be inserted for *set*, use a form of *to set*.

Example: Fried <u>chicken</u> <u>had been</u> (sat, <u>set</u>) in the basket.
                                                        (placed)

*In most cases

RISE/RAISE

To rise: means to go up (without help)
To raise: means to go up (with help)

FORMS:

Infinitive	Present	Past	Present Participle	(has, have, had) Past Participle
To rise	rise(s)	rose	rising	(had) risen
To raise	raise(s)	raised	raising	(had) raised

Two basic items for rise/raise:

A. To rise is an irregular verb; its forms need to be mastered.
   To raise is a regular verb.

B. *Raise* requires a direct object.*

Examples:

The sourdough bread is (rising, raising). There is no direct object so the
answer has to be *rising*.
The sourdough <u>bread is</u> (<u>rising,</u> raising).

The charity organization (rose, raised) money for the needy.

                                                           D.O.
The charity <u>organization</u> (rose, <u>raised</u>) money for the needy.

*<u>To raise</u> requires a direct object in most cases. However, there are exceptions.

    Example: The <u>flag</u> <u>had been</u> (risen, <u>raised</u>) at sunrise.

Keep in mind that *to raise* implies <u>with help</u>. The flag needed help; it could not have
gone up on its own. Therefore, *to raise* is correct even though there is no direct object
in the sentence.

60

LIE/LAY

To lie: means to rest or recline
To lay: means to place or to put

FORMS:

Infinitive	Present	Past	Present Participle	(has, have, had) Past Participle
To lie	lie(s)	lay	lying	(had) lain
To lay	lay(s)	laid	laying	(had) laid

Lie/lay is one of the most difficult concepts in English. The past tense of *to lie* and the present tense of *to lay* are the same.

Two basic items for lie/lay:

A. Lie/Lay are irregular verbs and <u>must be mastered</u>.

B. *Lay* will have a direct object.

    Examples:

        A pig is (lying, laying) in the mud.

        A <u>pig is</u> (<u>lying</u>, laying) ~~in the mud~~.   (There is no direct object in the sentence so the answer has to be *lying*.)

        We (lay, laid) the envelope on your desk yesterday.

                    D.O.

        We (lay, <u>laid</u>) the envelope ~~on your desk~~ yesterday.

                    (The object we laid on the desk was an envelope. Thus, envelope is a direct object.)

Directions: Cross out any prepositional phrases. Underline the subject once and the verb/verb phrase twice. Label any direct object(s)-<u>D.O.</u>

Reminder: <u>To Set/To Lay/To Raise</u> will have direct object(s).*

1.   She often (lies, lays) in the hammock to read.

2.   The farmer's daughter (rose, raised) a pig for her project.

3.   Candace (lay, laid) tile in the bathroom.

4.   Our mail was (lying, laying) on the kitchen counter.

5.   Have you (sat, set) there long?

6.   Every afternoon, the retired man (lies, lays) by the pool.

7.   The crowd (rose, raised) its voice in protest.

8.   Walter (sits, sets) his lunch by the door each evening.

9.   We had been (rising, raising) early.

10.   Father (lay, laid) the infant in the crib.

11.   Your paper is (lying, laying) by the front door.

12.   She (sat, set) quietly on the red velvet chair.

13.   The volunteer fire company (rose, raised) money for a new engine.

14.   Aunt Robyn (sits, sets) for a daily meditation.

15.   The clerk (lay, laid) my package on the counter.

*Most of the time.

Name_____   **SIT/SET**
                                        LIE/LAY
Date _____   **RISE/RAISE**

Directions: Cross out any prepositional phrases. Underline the subject once and
               the verb/verb phrase twice. Label any direct object(s)-<u>D.O.</u>

Reminder: <u>To Set/To Lay/To Raise</u> will have direct object(s).
                                              D.O.
        Example: <u>They</u> <u>were</u> (rising, <u>raising</u>) their hands (to show) agreement.

1.   The race car driver (sat, set) the keys on the hood of the car.

2.   A gray horse was (lying, laying) in an open meadow.

3.   We (sit, set) down to eat lunch.

4.   Smoke (rose, raised) up the chimney.

5.   The baker (sat, set) the pie in the pantry.

6.   Applesauce bread was (rising, raising).

7.   Martin (sits, sets) his toothbrush in the medicine cabinet.

8.   The sun had (risen, raised) at six o'clock.

9.   Did Hannah (sit, set) the record for the long jump?

10.   Our spaniel has (lain, laid) in that spot all afternoon.

11.   My dance partner (sits, sets) next to me in science class.

12.   We (lay, laid) the records on the stereo cabinet.

13.   A famous clothes designer was (sitting, setting) among many guests.

14.   Prices of shoes and socks have (risen, raised) in the last year.

15.   Mother and Dad (lay, laid) towels by the pool.

IRREGULAR VERB *TO BE*

You need to **memorize** and **master** the conjugation of *to be*.

is, **am**, **are**, **was**, **were**, **be**, **being**, **been**

Present Tense:

Singular: **is** (The <u>boy</u> **is** nice.)

am (<u>I</u> **am** here.) ***Am*** is used only with the **I** pronoun.

Plural: **are** (The <u>classes</u> **are** interesting.)

Past Tense:

Singular: **was** (The <u>person</u> **was** alone.)

Plural: **were** (Some <u>loons</u> **were** on the lake.)

LINKING VERBS

Linking verbs DO NOT SHOW ACTION. They link the **subject** with a noun or pronoun, or they link the subject with an adjective (describing word).

Examples: His <u>mother</u> <u>is</u> an accountant.

The <u>winners</u> of the game <u>were</u> they in blue shirts.

<u>Mary</u> <u>became</u> sick after the high jump.

There are three easy aspects of linking verbs:

A. Linking verbs never show action.

B. Linking verbs always link the subject with something.

C. Linking verbs appear as a separate list.

The following list of linking verbs must be **memorized** and **mastered**:

*to feel	to become	to remain
to taste	to seem	to appear
to look	to sound	to stay
to smell	to grow	to be (is, am, are, was, were, be, being, been)

To check if a verb (other than *to be*) is serving as a linking verb in a sentence, replace the verb with a form of *to be*. If the sentence makes sense and the meaning is not changed, the verb serves as a linking verb.

Examples: Joe seemed angry today.

<u>Joe</u> <u>was</u> angry today.

*High-utility linking verbs are included in this list.

LINKING VERBS

Predicate Nominative:

A **predicate nominative** is a noun (naming word) or a pronoun (I, he, she, we, they, who, you, or it) that is the <u>same as the subject of the sentence</u>. **Predicate nominative = P.N.**

                                    P.N.
Examples: My <u>dad</u> <u>is</u> the track coach at school.
                                    P.N.
           Ms. Brody <u>became</u> our teacher.

Predicate nominatives are easy to check. Simply invert the sentence starting with the word after the verb in a declarative sentence, tag on the verb, and add the complete subject. (Rather than going through all of the preceeding explanation, simply instruct students to "invert" the sentence and give many examples. Students quickly understand this process.)
                                    P.N.
Example: My <u>dad</u> <u>is</u> the track coach at school.

   Check: <u>The track coach at school is my dad</u>.

If a form of *to be* does not appear as the linking verb in the sentence, you will need to replace the existing linking verb with an appropriate form of *to be*.

Example: <u>Ms. Brody</u> <u>became</u> our teacher.

          Ms. Brody was our teacher.

   Check: <u>Our teacher was Ms. Brody</u>.

A sentence may contain a compound predicate nominative.
                          P.N.   P.N.
Example: My best <u>subjects</u> <u>are</u> history and math.

   Check: <u>History and math are my best subjects</u>.

66

LINKING VERBS

Predicate Nominatives:

In an interrogative sentence, the predicate nominative may be more difficult to find. Follow this method: turn the question into a statement, mark the sentence (subject, verb, and predicate nominative), and "invert" the statement to check it.

Example: Is Hannah the girl in the striped blouse?

P.N.

Hannah is the girl in the striped blouse.

Check: The girl in the striped blouse is Hannah.

Example: Are you the new secretary for student council?

P.N.

You are the new secretary for student council.

Check: The new secretary is* you.

*Sometimes the present form of *to be* (is, am, are) must be inserted when checking for predicate nominatives.

Example: Was Ralph the last person to see him?

P.N.

Ralph was the last person to see him.

Check: The last person to see him was Ralph.

Example: Did your nephew become a doctor?

P.N.

Your nephew did become a doctor.

Check: The doctor was your nephew. Was the doctor your nephew?

67

Directions: Cross out any prepositional phrases. Underline the subject once and the verb/verb phrase twice. Label the predicate nominative(s) in each sentence. Then, write the inverted form of the sentence on the line provided.

                                                   P.N.
Example: My brother is the boy ~~in the first row~~.

   Check: _____The boy is my brother._____

1.   Monica was the winner of the contest.

   _____

2.   My favorite food is pie.

   _____

3.   Our doctor was Dr. Strom.

   _____

4.   Their dessert was a banana split.

   _____

5.   My cousin is Freddy.

   _____

6.   Jane became my favorite aunt.

   _____

7.   The swimmers were Beth and her friend.

   _____

8.   My dog remained my pal throughout life.

   _____

9.   Ms. Armstrong is the speaker today.

   _____

10.   Bill has been our neighbor for years.

   _____

LINKING VERBS

Predicate Adjectives:

A predicate adjective is a **describing word** that occurs **after the verb** and goes back to describe the **subject** of the sentence.

In order for a word to be a predicate adjective, you must have the following:

    A. The sentence must contain a linking verb.
    B. The adjective must go back and describe the subject of the sentence.

                                  P.A.
  Examples: My <u>wagon</u> <u>is</u> red.   (red wagon)

                       P.A.
  The <u>man</u> <u>felt</u>* sick.   (sick man)

                           P.A.
  Sharp <u>cheese</u> <u>tastes</u> good. (good cheese)

                                P.A.
  <u>Birds</u> ~~in our backyard~~ <u>sounded</u> happy.   (happy birds)

Note: In the sentence, "John wore a blue shirt.", blue is NOT a predicate adjective. The verb *wore* is NOT a linking verb, and blue describes the shirt, NOT the subject, John.

Compound Predicate Adjectives:

  There may be more than one predicate adjective in a sentence.
                         P.A. P.A.   P.A.
  Examples: Our <u>flag</u> <u>is</u> red, white, and blue.   (red flag)

                                            (white flag)

                                            (blue flag)

                                  P.A.   P.A.
  The tired <u>child</u> <u>became</u> sleepy and restless.

                                         (sleepy child)

                                         (restless child)

---

*Remember that an aid to checking if the verb is linking is to see if you can insert a form of *to be* for the verb. If you can, the verb generally will be a linking verb. (The <u>man</u> <u>felt</u> (<u>was</u>) sick.)

Name_____   **LINKING VERBS**
                                        Predicate Adjectives
Date_____

Directions: Cross out any prepositional phrases. Underline the subject once and the
              verb/verb phrase twice. Label the predicate adjective(s) in each
              sentence. On the line after the sentence, write the predicate adjective(s)
              with the subject.
                                        P.A.
              Example: My <u>dog</u> <u>is</u> brown. _____brown dog_____

1.   Our tractor is yellow.   _____

2.   Sandpaper usually feels rough to the touch.   _____

3.   After the verdict, her face grew pale.   _____

4.   His plan sounded superb. _____

5.   That person certainly looks suspicious to me.   _____

6.   The dress in the closet was once purple.   _____

7.   Your lasagna tastes spicy. _____

8.   Hair should be soft and shiny.   _____

9.   The motorist seemed unaware of the accident._____

10.   Grandpa grows tired easily.   _____

11.   Their friends remained tense throughout the entire movie.   _____

      _____

12.   The cookies smelled burned.   _____

13.   The customer had become angry quickly.   _____

14.   Those plums were delicious.   _____

15.   The baby stayed happy during the entire shopping trip._____

70

ACTION OR LINKING VERBS

Some verbs can serve both as action and linking verbs.

Example: Joan <u>tasted</u> the soup. (action)

This drink <u>tastes</u> bitter. (linking)

Suggestion: **Insert a form of *to be* (is, am, are, was, were) for the verb. If the sentence meaning is not changed, the verb is usually linking.**

Examples: Joan <u>tasted</u> the soup.

Joan was the soup. (*Tasted* is not a linking verb here. The sentence meaning is changed by inserting *was.*)

This drink <u>tastes</u> bitter.

This drink is bitter. (*Tastes* is a linking verb. In inserting *is*, the sentence meaning is not changed.)

What <u>became</u> of him?

What was of him? (*Became* is not a linking verb here. Inserting *was* changes the sentence meaning.)

Directions: Cross out any prepositional phrases. Underline the subject once and the verb/verb phrase twice. Place an <u>A</u> on the line if the verb shows action. Place <u>L</u> on the line if the verb is linking. Above linking verbs, write a form of *to be* (*is, am, are, was, were*) as a check.

was

Example: __L__   Despite the medicine, the <u>patient</u> <u>remained</u> ill.

1. _____   The diner choked on a piece of steak.

2. _____   Suzanne grew excited about her new career.

3. _____   An insect bit me.

4. _____   His eyes looked glazed.

5. _____   We smelled the flowers.

6. _____   The mother looked at the messy house with displeasure.

7. _____   Your taco smells good.

8. _____   The electrician seemed sad about your decision.

9. _____   The seventh grader grew four inches during the summer.

10. _____   We tasted several strange foods at the international restaurant.

11. _____   The custodian felt his way down a darkened hall.

12. _____   The puppy stayed little for nearly a year.

13. _____   Melissa threw the ball to the pitcher.

14. _____   Our family felt happy about our new canary.

15. _____   Missionaries from Africa stayed with me for a week.

SUBJECT-VERB AGREEMENT

If the subject is singular (only one), the verb will be singular. In a **regular verb** (one that adds **ed** to form past time, e.g. walk/ walked), you add **s** to the verb when the subject is singular.

       Examples: Our maid cleans the room.

                 My father works hard.

                 The teller counts the money.

In most **irregular verbs**, the same rule applies. Simply add **s** to the verb.

       Examples: The runner breaks a record.

                 A thief steals a car.

                 He speaks well.

In a few irregular verbs, **es** is added to the verb.

       Examples: The baby goes to sleep early.

                 Mother teaches an exercise class.

VERBS
Subject-Verb Agreement

Directions: Cross out any prepositional phrases. Underline the subject once and the verb twice.

1.   The dentist (clean, cleans) my teeth during my yearly visit.

2.   My grandmother (plant, plants) tulips in her garden.

3.   After lunch our family (plan, plans) to go to the store.

4.   In biology class, Susan (sit, sits) beside me.

5.   Every afternoon the swimmer (dive, dives) into the pool.

6.   She (change, changes) a flat tire easily.

7.   A friend of my mother's (collect, collects) dolls.

8.   The worker (drive, drives) onto the freeway on the way to his job.

9.   That restaurant (serve, serves) lunch from noon until five o'clock.

10.   The bird (hop, hops) by the water fountain during the morning.

11.   Near the furniture factory (live, lives) a hobo with his dog.

12.   Our brother (pretend, pretends) to be a monster.

13.   Their niece (serve, serves) dessert after every dinner.

14.   Before a nap, that child (scream, screams) at the top of his lungs.

15.   A stack of old newspapers (stand, stands) on the porch.

SUBJECT-VERB AGREEMENT

If the subject is plural (more than one), do not add s to the verb.

Examples: Tigers (roam, roams) in the countryside.

Our trees (blossom, blossoms) in the spring.

In moot irregular verbs, you do not add s to the verb if the subject is plural.

Examples: The players (sit, sits) in the circle.

Her mother and she (swim, swims) every day.

If a compound subject (two or more) is joined by *or*, follow these rules:
A. If the subject closer to the verb is singular, add s to the verb.
Example: His daughters or **son** **needs** a ride home.

B. If the subject closer to the verb is plural, don't add s to the verb.
Example: His son or **daughters** **need** a ride home.

Directions: Cross out any prepositional phrases. Underline the subject once and the
correct verb twice.

1.   Three lawyers (comes, come) here for lunch.

2.   Margaret and her cousin (fly, flies) to Detroit each summer.

3.   Mary and Bill (arrives, arrive) at school before anyone.

4.   The women (eat, eats) here often.

5.   Tom's uncle (owns, own) a travel agency in our city

6.   Both the fifth grade team and the sixth grade team (win, wins) often.

7.   The new computers (works, work) well.

8.   They (hear, hears) weird sounds from the deserted shack.

9.   The tennis rackets (remain, remains) in the closet during the winter months.

10.   The hikers (walks, walk) ten miles a day.

11.   The members of our group (wants, want) a field trip to the museum.

12.   Spectators (line, lines) the streets for the Rose Bowl Parade.

13.   Horses and cows (lives, live) in the same barn.

14.   Firemen (practice, practices) CPR throughout their career.

15.   Father and Mother (leaves, leave) their offices early on Fridays.

Name_____   **VERBS**

Date_____

Directions: Cross out any prepositional phrases. Underline the subject once and the
verb/verb phrase twice.

Example: We packed and left for the cabin.

1.   Bob was leaving in a hurry.

2.   The clown jumped and nearly fell.

3.   Have you seen my books and notebook?

4.   The pitcher wants a starting position in the game.

5.   I had baked a pie and had eaten almost all of it by four o'clock.

6.   Ms. Brant's class might be going, too.

7.   The spider had spun an intricate web.

8.   She declared her innocence and then fainted.

9.   Should you have been given a larger size?

10.   Several square dancers will be performing at the rodeo.

11.   Jill is Greg's cousin.

12.   Has the librarian been reading that new book?

13.   You should have come with us to the parade.

14.   Grandma may be home now.

15.   I must finish or accept a last prize.

Directions: Cross out any prepositional phrases. Underline the subject once and the verb/verb phrase twice.

Example: The <u>gorilla</u> <u>has grown</u> rapidly.

1.   We cut out pictures and pasted them on large sheets of paper.

2.   Could you build a volcano for the science project?

3.   May the children wait until later in the week?

4.   Some teenagers are walking to the park to play tennis.

5.   He would not answer the question immediately.

6.   Some of the plants have withered and died during the night.

7.   Our judges will be selecting the grand prize winner in an hour.

8.   Several had never seen the Golden Gate Bridge.

9.   Alice's friend had ridden her bike to the store.

10.   The French toast will taste delicious with maple syrup.

11.   A beautiful model traveled to Sweden and appeared in a fashion show.

12.   The news reporter asked a few questions and then stated her opinion.

13.   Dad's office was broken into and robbed during the night.

14.   We wash our hair and brush our teeth at bedtime.

15.   Your grandpa should have been traveling with a companion.

Date_____

Directions: Cross out any prepositional phrases. Underline the subject once and the verb/verb phrase twice.

Example: Cars and trucks were stopped on the freeway.

1.   The boys scrambled up the ladder and scurried over the roof.

2.   Most of the candidates were not in attendance.

3.   The winter temperature may fall below zero in Chicago.

4.   The kids watched cartoons and then ate their lunch.

5.   Go to the store and get some bananas and detergent.

6.   The tiger leaped upon the truck and growled in the window.

7.   The cheerleader should have attended the workshop.

8.   The bunch of carrots was lying on the counter.

9.   Our family might have gone earlier that day.

10.   May he or she be permitted to delay the tournament for a day?

11.   The designer chose a fabric and then changed his mind.

12.   The students had gone to the auditorium and had sat quietly.

13.   The cyclist has traveled throughout Europe.

14.   Most of us must have done well on the examination.

15.   Cyrus cannot go to the movie or to the dance at school.

Directions: Cross out any prepositional phrases. Underline the subject once and the verb/verb phrase twice.

Example: The <u>package</u> <u>should</u> not <u>have been delivered</u> there.

1.   Was Bill leaving on the afternoon bus?

2.   Either Joan or Susan won the election.

3.   Sam crawled in the window and fell on the floor.

4.   That movie was good.

5.   Please go away.

6.   Shelly laughed then but cried later.

7.   Did Tom, Betty, or Heather recognize the burglar?

8.   One of the ladies left her purse and returned for it.

9.   He was vacationing in Brazil and found a peculiar rock.

10.   Neither the bananas nor the grapes have been eaten.

11.   He has been searching for the lost treasure of Tahiti.

12.   Stop and rest a few moments!

13.   The police, the nurses, and the sanitation workers have renewed their contracts.

14.   In these days of fast foods, we don't always remember our grandparents' hard labor in the kitchen.

15.   With guidance, the twins learned to tie their shoes and to write their names.

Date_____

Directions: Cross out any prepositional phrases. Underline the subject once and the verb/verb phrase twice.

Example: <u>Did</u> <u>you</u> <u>cut</u> the apple ~~into two pieces~~?

1. Neither Mary nor John has brought the homework.

2. When did the class leave for the field trip?

3. Glenn's dad was ill last week.

4. Were Pat and her nephew skiing last weekend?

5. That group of students should have eaten earlier in the day.

6. With clenched teeth, the determined wrestler grabbed his opponent and pinned him.

7. Either you must clean the garage or park your car in the street.

8. Go to the office, get some papers, and pass them out immediately.

9. Will some of the secretaries be going to lunch with us?

10. Each of the lawyers must take his work home with him.

11. Many men fought and died at the Alamo.

12. Within minutes, the team of basketball players finished and left.

13. Were the clowns or the trapeze artists funnier?

14. This is nice of you to go.

15. Both my foot and my leg had been injured in the accident.

16. You must go now or plan on spending the night.

17. Will any of the books be returned today?

18. Several ministers and deacons met and discussed church activities.

19. A hand-carved cradle had been made by her father's uncle.

20. Your pool should not have been cleaned before the storm.

VERB TENSES

Tenses mean time. Present tense, of course, signifies present time. Although present can mean "at this moment," it is easier to use the term, *today*, as a point of reference for present tense.

PRESENT TENSE NEVER HAS A HELPING (AUXILIARY) VERB.

1. If you know that the present tense never has a helper, you will not believe that the following sentence is present tense <u>although it sounds like the present tense</u>.

    The dog <u>is barking</u>.

    A. This sentence cannot be the present tense because there is a helping verb in the sentence. The entire verb phrase becomes *is barking*.

    B. The verb phrase, *is barking*, is actually a separate tense called the progressive tense.

2. To form the present tense, remove the *to* from the infinitive.

To speak = speak	(Today they speak.)
To talk = talk	(Today the boys talk.)
To push = push	(Today the vendors push the carts.)

Note that this holds true if the subject is plural (more than one).

To form the present tense with a singular subject, add <u>s</u> (and in some cases <u>es</u>) to the verb infinitive minus *to*.

To speak = speaks	(The guest speaks today.)
To talk = talks	(Today the boy talks.)
To push = pushes	(Today a vendor pushes his cart.)

VERB TENSES

PAST TENSE: Past tense indicates time that has occurred. Although past can

mean less than a second ago, it is easier to use the term,

yesterday, as a point of reference for past tense.

PAST TENSE NEVER HAS A HELPING (AUXILIARY) VERB.

1.   If you know that the past tense never has a helping verb, you will not believe that the following sentence is past tense.

Father <u>has gone</u>.

A. This sentence cannot be the past tense because there is a helping verb in the sentence. The entire verb phrase is *has gone*.

B. The verb phrase, *has gone*, is actually a separate tense called the perfect tense.

2.   To form the past tense, follow these two rules:

A. **To form the past tense of regular verbs, add <u>ed</u> to the verb.**

walk/walked   love/loved

B. **To form the past tense of irregular verbs, change the verb to its appropriate form.**

speak/spoke   bring/brought

FUTURE TENSE

Future tense indicates time yet to occur. It may be a second or a century from the moment.

There are two auxiliary (helping) verbs used with the future tense:

SHALL

WILL

Examples: I <u>shall go</u> to bed later.

<u>Will</u> Stan <u>go</u> with us tonight?

Note: Although it has become acceptable to use *will* with <u>any subject</u>, *shall* is generally reserved for the pronouns, *I* and *we*.

<u>THE FUTURE TENSE ALWAYS HAS THE HELPING VERBS WILL OR SHALL</u>.

Examples: The wind <u>will</u> probably <u>blow</u> hard tonight.

The dental assistant <u>will find</u> your chart.

<u>Shall</u> I <u>ask</u> for help?

Name_____ **VERBS**
                                          Tenses
Date_____

Directions: Cross out any prepositional phrases. Underline the subject once and the
              verb/verb phrase twice. Write present, past, or future in the space
              provided to indicate the sentence tense.

          Example: ____future____   The <u>cobbler</u> <u><u>will repair</u></u> my shoes.

1. _____   Some people persuade easily.

2. _____   We will persuade you to stay.

3. _____   My counselor persuaded me to attend college.

1. _____   It will seem lonely without you.

2. _____   That author seems lost in thought.

3. _____   The answer seemed unsuitable for the question.

1. _____   Arizona lies east of California.

2. _____   I will lie in the sun for ten minutes.

3. _____   The king lay on the royal bed.

1. _____   After playing, the children pick up all of their toys.

2. _____   Josh picked on other children constantly.

3. _____   Frances will pick you up after your appointment.

1. _____   Randy goes to ballet classes on Tuesday.

2. _____   Will you go with us?

3. _____   Our parents went to Hawaii this morning.

Name_____   **VERBS**
                                              Tenses
Date_____

Directions: Cross out any prepositional phrases. Underline the subject once and the
              verb/verb phrase twice. Write present, past, or future in the space
              provided to indicate the sentence tense.

    Example: ___present___   Some <u>workers</u> <u>want</u> higher wages.

1. _____   Small children often bring pets to school.

2. _____   One person will bring juice to the party.

3. _____   Susan brought her friends to church.

1. _____   Workmen delivered the furniture on Friday.

2. _____   Mother delivers speeches about safe driving.

3. _____   We will deliver your pizza in twenty minutes.

1. _____   I drink too much soda.

2. _____   A few cows drank water from the pond.

3. _____   The nutritionist will drink milk for lunch.

1. _____   My father enjoys letters to the editor.

2. _____   Will you enjoy the trip alone?

3. _____   The rock stars enjoyed the concert.

1. _____   Someone will write to you concerning the matter.

2. _____   The boss wrote a letter of explanation to his
                        employees.

3. _____   Tom and Sheila write well.

86

Name_____   **VERBS**
                                             Tenses
Date_____

Directions: In the space provided, place the required verb/verb phrase.

   Example: will paint   I (future of paint) later.

1. _____   Dinner (future of taste) good tonight.

2. _____   John (past of climb) a mountain.

3. _____   The horse (present of run) fast.

4. _____   The speaker (future of begin) soon.

5. _____   Some cars (past of break) down.

6. _____   Those girls (future of dance) for us.

7. _____   Everybody (past of laugh).

8. _____   Suzanne (present of knit) daily.

9. _____   We (past of fly) on TWA.

10. _____   School (future of be) over in June.

11. _____   Some (present of build) sand castles.

12. _____   A company (past of give) out balloons.

13. _____   I (past of choose) my partner.

14. _____   The sculptor (present of work) each day.

15. _____   The divers (past of crawl) to safety.

Name_____ **VERBS**

Temses

Date_____

Directions: In the space provided, place the required verb/verb phrase.

Example: _____is_____ Today (present of be) my birthday.

1. _____ Santa (future of come) on Christmas Eve.

2. _____ Martha (past of leave) her home at two o'clock.

3. _____ Barton (present of like) his new toy.

4. _____ Sharon (past of go) to her practice.

5. _____ They (present of bring) their mother here.

6. _____ Andrew (future of help) with the cleaning.

7. _____ The box (past of arrive) in April.

8. _____ I (future of buy) a new car.

9. _____ Laughter (past of ring) out.

10. _____ Alicia and he (present of be) my choices.

11. _____ The duck (past of swim) in the pond.

12. _____ Mountain climbers (future of try) again.

13. _____ Kathy (present of talk) constantly.

14. _____ The public pool (future of close) today.

15. _____ The constant noise (past of drive) me crazy.

88

PERFECT TENSE

The perfect tense uses the past participle form.

Perfect Tense = *to have* + past participle

To have:

Present:	have
	has
Past:	had
Future:	will have or shall have

Steps in forming the perfect tense:

1. Decide the past participle form of the given verb.

    Examples: to give = given   to place = placed

2. Decide the correct form of *to have*. If future perfect is required, use the future of *to have* (<u>will have</u>). Past perfect requires the past of *to have* (<u>had</u>). In forming the present perfect, either <u>have</u> or <u>has</u> will be used in order to make subject and verb agree.

3. Combine the *to have* form and the past participle form to make the perfect tense.

PERFECT TENSE (to know):

Present Perfect:	have known
	has known
Past Perfect:	had known
Future Perfect:	will have known or shall have known

Name_____   **VERBS**
                                               Perfect Tense
Date_____

Directions: Cross out any prepositional phrases. Underline the subject once and the
              verb/verb phrase twice. Write present perfect, past perfect, or future
              perfect in the space provided to indicate tense.

        Example: _present perfect_   John has read fifty books.

1.   _____   The truck had tipped over on its side.

2.   _____   She has tipped the waiter five dollars.

3.   _____   Within a few months, the informant will have
                                 provided the detectives with information.

1.   _____   By June, we will have flown across the Atlantic
                                 Ocean four times.

2.   _____   Have you ever flown in a DC-10?

3.   _____   Mother had flown to San Francisco on a
                                 business trip.

1.   _____   The track team has run the relay.

2.   _____   Had the winner run in a marathon before?

3.   _____   The Broadway show will have run for a year
                                 in August.

1.   _____   We will have nailed the entire fence by the
                                 end of the day.

2.   _____   Have you nailed the broken piece of wood to
                                 the cabinet?

3.   _____   Who had nailed in the golden spike for the
                                 transcontinental railroad?

Name_____ **VERBS**

Perfect Tense

Date_____

Directions: Cross out any prepositional phrases. Underline the subject once and the verb/verb phrase twice. Write present perfect, past perfect, or future perfect in the space provided to indicate tense.

1. _____ They have chosen an alternate route to St. Louis.

2. _____ Hopefully Janice and Paul will have chosen their course of study by fall.

3. _____ Five judges had chosen the finalists.

1. _____ Margaret has joined a softball league.

2. _____ Had the twins joined 4-H last year?

3. _____ After the wedding, the minister will have joined them in holy matrimony.

1. _____ By sunset, the motorist will have ridden five hundred miles.

2. _____ The excited children had ridden in a hot air balloon.

3. _____ Have you ever ridden in a Model T?

1. _____ Our package has arrived.

2. _____ All passengers will have arrived by noon.

3. _____ The baby had arrived safely.

1. _____ My grandfather had seen Teddy Roosevelt.

2. _____ We have already seen the fireworks display.

3. _____ By the end of the tour, our class will have seen most of Washington, D. C.

Directions: In the space provided, place the required verb phrase.

Example: __have seen_____   I (present perfect of see) him.

1. _____   The child (present perfect of see) me.

2. _____   His father (past perfect of see) it twice.

3. _____   Someone (future perfect of see) the page.

4. _____   Marvin and Greta (present perfect of break) a pitcher.

5. _____   The players (past perfect of break) a record.

6. _____   They (future perfect of break) the tie.

7. _____   The choir (past perfect of sing).

8. _____   My sister (future perfect of sing) by then.

9. _____   Often I (present perfect of sing) for them.

10. _____   The joggers (future perfect of run) a mile.

11. _____   A train (past perfect of run) out of steam.

12. _____   Number 4 (present perfect of run) in nearly every race.

13. _____   Some olives (past perfect of fall) from the tree.

14. _____   Cereal (present perfect of fall) on the floor.

15. _____   Ten inches of snow (future perfect of fall) by evening.

PROGRESSIVE TENSE

The progressive tense uses the present participle form.

> Progressive Tense = *to be* + present participle

To be:

Present:	am
	is
	are
Past:	was
	were
Future:	will be or shall be

Steps in forming the progressive tense:

1. Decide the present participle form of the given verb.

    Examples: to grow = growing   to yell = yelling

2. Decide the correct form of *to be*.

    A. Present progressive will use <u>is</u>, <u>am</u>, or <u>are</u> with the present participle.

    B. Past progressive will use <u>was</u> or <u>were</u> with the present participle.

    C. Future progressive will use <u>shall be</u> or <u>will be</u> with the present participle.

In forming the present progressive and past progressive, it is necessary to have subject and verb agreement.

Progressive Tense (to watch):

Present Progressive:	am watching
	is watching
	are watching
Past Progressive:	was watching
	were watching
Future Progressive:	will be watching or shall be watching

VERBS
Progressive Tense

Directions: Cross out any prepositional phrases. Underline the subject once and the verb/verb phrase twice. Write present progressive (pres. pro.), past progressive (past pro.), or future progressive (fut. pro.) to indicate the tense of the sentence.

Example: _past pro._____   A <u>swan</u> <u>was swimming</u> ~~across the lake~~.

1.   _____   A camel is lying along the road.

2.   _____   Meat loaf was baking in the oven.

3.   _____   We will be collecting cans this afternoon.

4.   _____   Monkeys are swinging in the trees.

5.   _____   A frisky rabbit was nibbling the lettuce.

6.   _____   Will our class be going on a field trip?

7.   _____   I am leaving for Europe tomorrow.

8.   _____   We will soon be learning how to etch glass.

9.   _____   The young girls were using different types of makeup.

10.   _____   Birds were eating crumbs in the yard.

11.   _____   Our club will be going there on Friday.

12.   _____   My lower lip is burning.

13.   _____   I am learning about yoga and karate.

14.   _____   The clown was dancing for the small children.

15.   _____   Are you keeping a journal?

VERBS
Progressive Tense

Directions: Cross out any prepositional phrases. Underline the subject once and the verb/verb phrase twice. Write present progressive (pres. pro.), past progressive (past pro.), or future progressive (fut. pro.) to indicate the tense of the sentence.

Example: <u>pres. pro.</u>   <u>They</u> <u>are listening</u> very carefully.

1. _____ Toys were lying all over the floor.

2. _____ The painter is adding the last few touches to our wall.

3. _____ Am I going, too?

4. _____ The sky was growing dark.

5. _____ Will I be choosing the best three essays?

6. _____ Are you telling me the truth?

7. _____ We will be hiking the canyon this month.

8. _____ Were you skiing at Aspen last winter?

9. _____ I am refinishing an antique chest.

10. _____ The company was not sharing its profits.

11. _____ Our family was camping last weekend.

12. _____ The lakes will be freezing during the winter months.

13. _____ Five families were having a garage sale.

14. _____ Smoke was rising from several chimneys.

15. _____ Will the cowboy artists be presenting any new works at the fall showing?

VERBS
Tenses

Directions: In the space provided, place the required verb/verb phrase.

Example: <u>spent</u>_____   We (past of spend) too much money.

1.   _____   Abigail (future of play) in the tennis tournament.

2.   _____   The girls (past of see) the large flag.

3.   _____   The children (present of act) in classroom plays.

4.   _____   Some flies (past of fly) around the honey.

5.   _____   Washington (past perfect of serve) two terms.

6.   _____   February (present perfect of arrive).

7.   _____   In track, the members (future progressive of run.)

8.   _____   Pontiac (past perfect of try) to unite the Indians.

9.   _____   We (future progressive of celebrate) your anniversary.

10.   _____   The dog (present of lie) on a mat.

11.   _____   Many students (future progressive of receive) good grades.

12.   _____   A few (future perfect of leave) by the time you arrive.

13.   _____   Joan (past perfect of buy) a card.

14.   _____   Joan (past of buy) a card.

15.   _____   Joan (past progressive of buy) a card.

96

VERBS

Transitive or Intransitive?

A TRANSITIVE VERB WILL HAVE A DIRECT OBJECT.

Direct Object = Transitive

D.O.T. or DOT is a very easy way to remember that a transitive verb will have a direct object.

Remember: **A direct object receives the action of the verb.**

Examples: The <u>child threw</u> the **ball**. (Ball is the direct object; ball is what the child threw.)

<u>Sally grabbed</u> the **broom** from me. (Broom is the direct object; broom is what Sally grabbed.)

AN INTRANSITIVE VERB WILL NOT HAVE A DIRECT OBJECT.

The <u>cat is</u> up on the sink. (Intransitive Verb - no direct object)

<u>We ran</u> after the ice cream truck. (Intransitive Verb - no direct object. Even though <u>ran</u> is an action verb, there is no direct object in the sentence.)

The <u>trees have been trimmed</u> today. (Intransitive Verb - no direct object)

Directions: Cross out any prepositional phrases. Underline the subject once and the
verb/verb phrase twice. Circle the direct object(s).

Example: He paid **cash** for the groceries.

1.   The dentist gave sugarless lollipops to his young patients.

2.   You left your keys in this drawer.

3.   Brad grabbed his coat from the front closet.

4.   Jerry gave a corsage to his mother for Mothers' Day.

5.   We cooked bacon and eggs for breakfast.

6.   A nurse lifted the baby into her arms.

7.   Have you ever eaten artichokes?

8.   An investor bought land in Colorado.

9.   The bachelor bought towels for his new apartment.

10.   Pat poured juice into fancy, pink glasses.

11.   I have given the waitress a large tip.

12.   The custodian lowered the flag after school.

13.   They ride their bikes on the sidewalk.

14.   Peter climbs the tree often.

15.   Hang the pictures on that wall.

VERBS

Transitive or
Intransitive?

Directions: Cross out any prepositional phrases. Underline the subject once and the verb/verb phrase twice.

Write the direct object of the sentence in the space provided. If there is no direct object, write none in the space provided. Then circle T if the verb is transitive and I if the verb is intransitive.

Remember: Transitive verbs have direct objects. (D.O.T.)
Intransitive verbs do not have direct objects.

Example: ___foot___ (T) I 1. I broke my foot.

_____ T I 1. The senior ate three doughnuts for breakfast.

_____ T I 2. Have you washed any cars lately?

_____ T I 3. The fireworks display was spectacular.

_____ T I 4. I burned my finger on the iron.

_____ T I 5. Mother was given five rides on that camel.

_____ T I 6. Eggs were cracked into a large bowl.

_____ T I 7. Flour had been ground for the griddle cakes.

_____ T I 8. At the end of recess, a teacher blows a whistle.

_____ T I 9. The curtains have not been chosen.

_____ T I 10. My sandals are of fine quality leather.

_____ T I 11. Priscilla flew in a helicopter to the building site.

_____ T I 12. A cook's helper grated cheese for a salad.

_____ T I 13. Your title is not centered on the page.

_____ T I 14. Go!

_____ T I 15. That tour group will take a train to Boise, Idaho.

Name_____   **VERBS**
                                          Transitive or
Date_____   Intransitive?

Directions: Cross out any prepositional phrases. Underline the subject once and the
               verb/verb phrase twice. Place a T in the space provided if the verb is
               transitive. Place an I in the space provided if the verb is intransitive.

          Example: T   1.   The captain gave me a tour of the ship.

Remember: A transitive verb has a direct object.

_____   1.   The Mississippi River flows into the Gulf of Mexico.

_____   2.   Go away!

_____   3.   I threw the crumpled paper in the trash.

_____   4.   Those trees had been planted early in the century.

_____   5.   Stella placed the vacuum cleaner in the middle of the living
                        room.

_____   6.   We planted geraniums in the flower bed.

_____   7.   Those huskies are trained to attack.

_____   8.   This house has three fire alarms.

_____   9.   Phil threw the ball into the neighbor's yard.

_____   10.   Some crumbs had been thrown to the birds.

_____   11.   Do you ever buy Indian jewelry?

_____   12.   An antique dealer bought four porcelain mugs at the sale.

_____   13.   The telephone rang for several minutes and then stopped.

_____   14.   She carries her lunch in a small yellow bag.

_____   15.   Our slides of Japan have been shown many times.

INDIRECT OBJECTS

An indirect object is the receiver of some direct objects.

Example: Mother baked **me** a cake.
(D.O. above "a cake")

Rules for an Indirect Object:

1. **In order to have an indirect object in a sentence, there must be a direct object.**

Example: Bill baked my mother some brownies.
(I.O. above "my mother", D.O. above "some brownies")

2. **You can mentally insert *to* or *for* before an indirect object.**

Examples: A. Bill baked **for** / my mother brownies.

B. The carrier handed **to** / the lady a newspaper.

Note: If <u>to</u> or <u>for</u> is actually written in the sentence, the noun or pronoun that follows is <u>NOT</u> an indirect object.

Examples: A. He gave <u>to Martha</u> his umbrella.

(<u>Martha</u> is not an indirect object.)

B. Ms. Martin received <u>for her neighbors</u> their vacation mail.

(<u>Neighbors</u> is not an indirect object.)

3. **A sentence containing a direct object does not have to contain an indirect object.**

Examples: Did they send flowers? (No indirect object)
(D.O. above "flowers")

Did they send the **winner** flowers? (Indirect Object)
(I.O. above "winner", D.O. above "flowers")

4. **Compound indirect objects may occur in sentences.**

Examples: A clown gave **Teresa** and **Donald** balloons.
(I.O. above "Teresa", I.O. above "Donald", D.O. above "balloons")

The chef prepared **Larry** and his **date** a meal.
(I.O. above "Larry", I.O. above "date", D.O. above "a meal")

Directions: Cross out any prepositional phrases. Underline the subject once and the verb/verb phrase twice. Label the indirect object(s) I.O. and the direct object(s) D.O. in the following sentences.

                                                                  I.O.   D.O.
Example: A <u>seamstress</u> <u>made</u> Frances Ann a flower girl dress.

1.   We sent the company proofs of purchase for a free frisbee.

2.   Jackie ordered her husband a stereo for their anniversary.

3.   The collector gave us three new garbage cans.

4.   The child draws his parents pretty pictures at school.

5.   The loan officer has often loaned them money.

6.   Will you send the shop owner my new address?

7.   Has the rental agent found the young couple an apartment?

8.   Each year the boss gives the employees a cash bonus.

9.   I gave Terry your books after the class.

10.   A gypsy had told Harriet an unusual story.

11.   Don't give anyone our tickets.

12.   She baked the family a pie.

13.   Can you hand me your paper?

14.   Someone ordered Mr. Jones and Mrs. Herb spark plugs for their Model T.

15.   The termite inspector should have told us more information.

Date_____

Directions: Decide where the indirect object is in each sentence. Place a
          / <u>to</u> or a / <u>for</u> where <u>to</u> or <u>for</u> should be inserted mentally.
                    to
          Example: We sent / Marshall shells from Florida.

1.   That cashier gave Dr. King some change.

2.   I prepared them a huge feast.

3.   My friend sent you the proper forms.

4.   Dad presented me a bike for my birthday.

5.   The artist drew our company a sketch of the new building.

6.   The librarian presented the child a reading award.

7.   Laura asked the teacher a question.

8.   A missionary gave the natives food.

9.   Her company printed the customer twenty business cards.

10.   The traffic officer presented the driver a speeding ticket.

11.   Dad bakes us cookies every Tuesday afternoon.

12.   I handed the teller five checks.

13.   The corporation owner gives that charity organization a large donation
       each year.

14.   Grandpa sent Rick and Barbara chocolate chip cookies at camp.

15.   He fixed us a place to sleep for the night.

Directions: Cross out any prepositional phrases. Underline the subject once and the
verb/verb phrase twice. Label the indirect object I.O. and the direct object
D.O.

                                    I.O.   D.O.
Example: We sent Marshall shells from Florida.

1.   That cashier gave Dr. King some change.

2.   I prepared them a huge feast.

3.   My friend sent you the proper form.

4.   Dad presented me a bike for my birthday.

5.   The artist drew our company a sketch of the new building.

6.   The librarian presented the child a reading award.

7.   Laura asked the teacher a question.

8.   A missionary gave the natives food.

9.   Her company printed the customer twenty business cards.

10.   The traffic officer presented the driver a speeding ticket.

11.   Dad bakes us cookies every Tuesday afternoon.

12.   I handed the teller five checks.

13.   The corporation owner gives that charity organization a large donation
each year.

14.   Grandpa sent Rick and Barbara chocolate chip cookies at camp.

15.   He fixed us a place to sleep for the night.

Date_____

A. Contractions:
Directions: Write the contraction.

1. they will - _____   6. I have - _____

2. it is - _____   7. should not - _____

3. had not - _____   8. cannot - _____

4. we are - _____   9. they are - _____

5. does not - _____   10. what is - _____

B. Auxiliary (Helping) Verbs:
Directions: Write the 23 auxiliary verbs.

_____

_____

_____

C. Verb Phrases:
Directions: Cross out any prepositional phrases. Underline the subject once and the verb/verb phrase twice. Write the helping (auxiliary) verb(s) in the first column and the main verb in the second column.

HELPING VERB(S)   MAIN VERB

1. He must have tripped on a rock.   _____ _____

2. A dentist should examine your teeth._____ _____

3. May I purchase a ticket for a ride?   _____ _____

4. During the game, the player
   should have listened to the coach.   _____ _____

5. The lady with the small child will
   not be remaining at the meeting.   _____ _____

6. Does anyone want to go along?   _____ _____

D. **Irregular Verbs Using Direct Objects:**
    Directions: Cross out any prepositional phrases. Underline the subject once
                 and the verb/verb phrase twice. Label any direct object-<u>D.O.</u>

1. Penny (sits, sets) her books on the kitchen table.

2. Their dog was (lying, laying) near the front door.

3. That majorette (rose, raised) her baton to begin her routine.

4. During the assembly, please (sit, set) beside the exit.

5. The girls have (laid, lain) by the pool for one-half hour.

6. With a look of relief, Joshua (sat, set) the packages in the van.

7. Dough for onion bread (rises, raises) in a very warm place.

E. **Linking Verbs:**
    Directions: List the linking verbs (12 infinitives + 8).

_____

_____

F. **Linking or Action Verbs?:**
    Directions: Cross out any prepositional phrases. Underline the subject once
                 and the verb/verb phrase twice.   Write <u>A</u> in the space if the verb is
                 action.   Write <u>L</u> in the space if the verb is linking.
Remember: **Write *is*, *am*, *are*, *was*, or *were* above a verb that you think is linking. If
              the meaning of the sentence is not changed, the verb is usually linking.**

1. _____ Orange blossoms smell very fragrant.

2. _____ Jordan's cousin seems very nice.

3. _____ Billie swept the floor after dinner.

4. _____ That curvy road looks dangerous.

5. _____ The baker tasted a sample of cheesecake.

G. **Linking Verbs/Predicate Adjectives:**
Directions: Cross out any prepositional phrases. Underline the subject once
and the verb twice. Write <u>Yes</u> if the boldfaced word is a predicate
adjective; write <u>No</u> if the boldfaced word isn't a predicate adjective.

Remember: Be sure to determine if the sentence contains a linking verb.

1. _____   This blanket feels **scratchy**.

2. _____   Dawn and Jack baked a **delicious** pie.

3. _____   That cut on your arm looks **painful**.

4. _____   They looked in the **antique** chest for a picture album.

5. _____   His voice sounded **faint** from a distance.

H   **Linking Verbs/Predicate Nominatives:**
Directions: Place the predicate nominative in the space provided. Then,
rewrite the sentence to prove it. If there is no predicate nominative,
write <u>none</u>.

Remember: Be sure to determine if the sentence contains a linking verb.

1. _____   His favorite city is Chicago.

    Proof: _____

2. _____   The leader of the Continental Army was
                                     George Washington.

    Proof: _____

3. _____   Mr. Thorton handed a paper to Danny.

    Proof: _____

4. _____   Sally Kenton became the club's secretary.

    Proof: _____

Date_____

I. **Subject/Verb Agreement:**
Directions: Cross out any prepositional phrases. Underline the subject once and the verb/verb phrase twice. Be sure that the subject and verb agree.

1. Margaret's jump rope (is, are) on the floor.

2. Those acrobats (perform, performs) often.

3. The store manager and a clerk (counts, count) the money at closing time.

4. Geese (fly, flies) south for the winter.

5. One of the mail carriers (live, lives) in Katie's neighborhood.

6. Everyone without a partner (need, needs) to go to the end of the line.

J. **Tenses:**
Directions: Cross out any prepositional phrases. Underline the subject once and the verb/verb phrase twice. In the space provided, write the tense: *present*, *past*, or *future*.

1. _____   A letter regarding the new library is on the desk.

2. _____   The meeting will be after dinner.

3. _____   Shall I open this envelope from the insurance company?

4. _____   His mother placed the ladder against the house.

5. _____   Two eagles soared above the trees.

6. _____   All of Brian's relatives live in Toledo, Ohio.

108

Date_____

K.   **Past Participles:**

Directions: Write the past participle form.

1.   to bring - _____   6.   to swim - _____

2.   to leave - _____   7.   to lie - _____

3.   to spring - _____   8.   to ride - _____

4.   to eat - _____   9.   to wear - _____

5.   to do - _____   10.   to shake - _____

L.   **Verb Phrases/Irregular Verbs:**

Directions: Cross out any prepositional phrases. Underline the subject once
            and the verb/verb phrase twice.

1.   Snow had (fallen, fell) during the night.

2.   Smoke has (rose, risen) from the campfire.

3.   After church, their family had (went, gone) to a friend's house.

4.   Claudia and Michael were (chose, chosen) for the play.

5.   Has the bell (rang, rung) yet?

6.   The banana peels had been (threw, thrown) into the garbage.

7.   A passenger must have (taken, took) the last seat on the bus.

8.   Marsh and his dad had (ran, run) a mile before breakfast.

9.   Awards were (gave, given) to each contestant.

10.   Wind had (blown, blew) through the valley for several days.

M.   **Tenses:**

>   Directions: Cross out any prepositional phrases.   Underline the subject once
>   and the verb phrase twice.   Write the tense in the space provided.

Be specific. Your answer will be one of the following: *present perfect*, *past perfect*,
future perfect, *present progressive*, *past progressive*, or *future progressive*.

1.   _____   The carpenter in the red truck had
                                         forgotten his tools.

2.   _____   A dance student is purchasing new
                                         ballet shoes.

3.   _____   Have you decided about your summer
                                         plans?

4.   _____   Several boys were yelling to their
                                         friends.

5.   _____   By March, I shall have earned
                                         enough money for a bicycle.

6.   _____   Will you be eating in the dining room?

N.   **Verb Phrases:**

>   Directions: Cross out any prepositional phrases. Underline the subject once
>   and the verb/verb phrase twice.

1.   One of June's cousins has decided to be a dental hygienist.

2.   Shouldn't Bianca have taken those yellow plastic bags with her?

3.   Is the bus driver returning to the bus garage after her last stop?

4.   In May, electric car races will be held at a nearby raceway.

5.   Cut this meat into small pieces and coat it with flour for stew.

A. Prepositions:

Directions: Write fifty prepositions.

1. _____	14. _____	27. _____	40. _____
2. _____	15. _____	28. _____	41. _____
3. _____	16. _____	29. _____	42. _____
4. _____	17. _____	30. _____	43. _____
5. _____	18. _____	31. _____	44. _____
6. _____	19. _____	32. _____	45. _____
7. _____	20. _____	33. _____	46. _____
8. _____	21. _____	34. _____	47. _____
9. _____	22. _____	35. _____	48. _____
10. _____	23. _____	36. _____	49. _____
11. _____	24. _____	37. _____	50. _____
12. _____	25. _____	38. _____	
13. _____	26. _____	39. _____	

B. Prepositions in sentences:

Directions: Cross out any prepositional phrases. Underline the subject and the
verb/verb phrase twice.

1.   After a long day with many clients, the lawyer left her office for another meeting.

2.   One of the professors spoke about his studies at a French university.

3.   Take the bus along Hearn Road to arrive near a shopping center.

the cook
the President
Proper Nouns
none Mr. Jones
Adam
Pronouns
he I me
they your

CONCRETE AND ABSTRACT NOUNS

A noun names a person, a place, or a thing.

(Concrete) **nouns usually can be seen:** book, car, chair, hammer, towel, store

Some concrete nouns you technically won't be able to see unless they are examined in very small parts (atoms). Examples: air, wind, breath

(Abstract) **nouns are those that cannot be seen:** love, liberty, grace, sadness

To test if a word might be an abstract noun, do the following:

A. Check to see that the possible noun doesn't describe any word in the sentence. If it does, STOP. It's a describing word called an adjective.

   Example: A <u>love</u> gift was collected for the needy.

   In this sentence, <u>love</u> is an adjective that describes gift. Thus <u>love</u> is an adjective and not a noun in this sentence.

B. If the possible noun does not qualify as an adjective, try placing "the" in front of it. If you can put "the" in front of the possible noun, the word is probably a noun.

   Example: A very special moment is sharing <u>love</u> with a pet.

   You can say "the love" in this sentence, so love is a noun.

NOUNS
Concrete or Abstract?

Directions: In the space provided, place <u>C</u> if the noun is concrete and <u>A</u> if the noun is abstract.

1. ___A___ loyalty
2. ___C___ guitar
3. ___C___ spoon
4. ___A___ kindness
5. ___A___ joy
6. ___C___ cereal
7. ___A___ patience
8. ___C___ clock
9. ___A___ friendship
10. ___C___ boots
11. ___A___ hatred
12. ___C___ smoke
13. ___A___ gentleness
14. ___C___ door
15. ___C___ ears
16. ___A___ peace
17. ___C___ forest
18. ___A___ liberty
19. ___A___ anger
20. ___C___ rabbit
21. ___A___ fear
22. ___C___ pie
23. ___A___ wisdom
24. ___C___ cream
25. ___A___ beauty

NOUNS

Nouns name persons, places, things, or ideas.

Sometimes the same word will be a noun in one sentence and an adjective (describing word) in another sentence.

Examples: A. The <u>candle</u> was blown out by the wind.

(Candle is a <u>noun</u> in this sentence.)

The <u>candle</u> holder was broken.

(Candle is an adjective because it describes holder in this sentence.)

B. Our <u>desk</u> is a mess.

(Desk is a <u>noun</u> in this sentence. It names a thing.)

This <u>desk</u> lamp is in need of repair.

(Desk is an adjective because it describes lamp in this sentence.)

Sometimes the same word will be a noun in one sentence and a verb in another sentence.

Examples: The <u>park</u> is nearby.

(*Park* is a <u>noun</u> in this sentence.)

<u>Park</u> the car.

(*Park* is a <u>verb</u> in this sentence.)

114

Name_____

Date_____

Directions: On the line provided, write N. if the underlined word is a noun or ADJ. if the word is an adjective (describing word).

1.   _____N_____   Don't break that <u>glass</u>.

2.   _____A_____   Your <u>glass</u> vase is very expensive.

3.   _____Adj_____   Her <u>flower</u> garden is in full bloom.

4.   _____N_____   My mother gave me a <u>flower</u> for my birthday.

5.   _____N_____   We often take <u>pictures</u> on vacation.

6.   _____ADJ_____   Do you have a <u>picture</u> compartment in your wallet?

7.   _____N_____   Those children are filing their <u>nails</u>.

8.   _____ADJ_____   A <u>nail</u> file was lying on the floor.

9.   _____A_____   John made a great <u>paper</u> airplane.

10.   _____N_____   The <u>papers</u> were passed to the ones in the last row.

11.   _____N_____   An assortment of <u>baskets</u> hung on the wall.

12.   _____A_____   <u>Basket</u> weaving is an enjoyable activity.

13.   _____N_____   Have you read this <u>book</u>?

14.   _____A_____   New <u>book</u> mobile units were purchased by the library.

15.   _____N_____   Jimmy has a new <u>wagon</u>.

16.   _____A_____   A <u>wagon</u> load of hay was pulled by the oxen.

17.   _____N_____   The group listened to many <u>tapes</u> about life.

18.   _____A_____   Several <u>tape</u> players were on sale.

19.   _____A_____   <u>Peanut</u> shells lay all over the floor.

20.   _____N_____   A <u>peanut</u> is high in protein.

NOUNS

A.   Articles: **a, an, the**

B.   Demonstratives: **this, that, those, these**

C.   Numbers

D.   Possessive Adjectives (also called possessive pronouns used as adjectives)

E.   Possessive Nouns (used as adjectives)

F.   Indefinites: **some, few, many, several, no, any***

A. **A, an,** and **the** will come before a noun and sometimes a pronoun. The noun may have another word in front of it, but a noun will be in the vicinity of **a, an,** and **the**.

Examples: **a** <u>book</u>   **the** <u>movie</u>   **an** <u>orange</u>   **a** lovely <u>scene</u>

B. The demonstratives, **this, that, those, these,** MAY be signals for a noun to follow. However, sometimes they stand alone.

Examples: **this** <u>book</u>   **that** <u>light</u>   **those** <u>buttons</u>   **these** <u>cars</u>

NOTE: If any demonstrative does NOT have a person, place, or thing closely following it, that particular demonstrative will not be a determiner.

Examples: This is fun.   (<u>This</u> stands alone; <u>this</u> is NOT a determiner.)

I like those.   (<u>Those</u> stands alone; <u>those</u> is NOT a determiner.)

C. Numbers may signal a noun. STOP and check if a person, place, or thing follows the number(s). Describing words often come between the number and the noun.

Examples: **Fifty-one** <u>people</u>   **seven** white <u>ducklings</u>

NOTE: If a number does NOT have a person, place, or thing after it, the number will NOT serve as a determiner for a noun.

Example: Three stayed behind. (<u>Three</u> stands alone; <u>three</u> is not a determiner.)

*This list is incomplete.

D. Possessive Pronouns (used as adjective determiners):

my, his, her, our, their, its, your

These often signal a noun. When you see one of these determiners, STOP! Check if a word naming a person, place, or thing is following. **My, its, your, our,** and **their** will be followed by a noun.

Examples: **my** hair   **your** key   **our** new radio

its tail   **their** short trip

Examples:

Her ankle was broken.   (Ankle is a noun signaled by **her**.)

Did you go with her?   (Her does not go to a word naming a person, place, or thing.)

E. Possessive nouns often signal other nouns. Look for a word naming a person, place, or thing after any posssessive noun.

Examples: **Craig's** canoe   **bank's** hours   **visitor's** parking

F. Indefinites:

some, any, no, many, few, several

Indefinites are determiners when a noun follows. Upon seeing an indefinite, check to determine if a noun follows it. A describing word may fall between an indefinite and the noun.

Example: **Some** putty knives were lying on the counter.

(Knives is a noun signaled by **some**.)

Example: Some of the newspapers were thrown away.

(Cross out the prepositional phrase of the newspapers. You have left: Some were thrown away. There is no noun after some.)

NOUN DETERMINERS

Although noun determiners are actually adjectives, it is better to simply call them determiners. Determiners are stop signals. When you see a determiner, <u>stop</u>! Determiners signal that a noun or pronoun may follow. Closely examine the sentence and decide if a noun (or pronoun) is following the determiner.

<u>Classification of Determiners</u>:

A. Articles: **a, an, the**

B. Demonstratives: **this, that, those, these**

C. Numbers (**ten** ducks)

D. Possessive adjectives (also called possessive pronouns used as adjectives)

     my, his, her, your, its, our, their

E. Possessive nouns (used as adjectives): (**Jack's** net) (**fly's** wing)

F. Indefinites: **some, few, many, several, no, any***

Examples:

       NOUN   NOUN

My kite sailed high above **the** roof tops.   <u> my kite   </u>

                                         <u> the tops   </u>

           NOUN   NOUN

Lori's suede shoes have **many** holes.   <u>Lori's shoes </u>

                                         <u>many holes </u>

       NOUN   NOUN

Two chipmunks are playing under **that** bush.   <u>two chipmunks</u>

                                         <u> that bush   </u>

        NOUN

A tourist's camera is usually important.   <u> a camera   </u>

                                         <u>tourist's camera</u>

*There are other indefinites.

NOUNS
Determiners

Directions: In the space provided, write the underlined determiner with the noun that it modifies.

Example: I swam in <u>the</u> lake today.   _____the lake_____

1. <u>My</u> family has gone fishing.   _____

2. Have you received <u>Ann's</u> letter?   _____

3. <u>Several</u> small squirrels played.   _____

4. I like <u>these</u> posters on your wall.   _____

5. <u>A</u> snow cone is refreshing.   _____

6. <u>His</u> old, black hat is a favorite.   _____

7. Do you have <u>any</u> peppermint candy?   _____

8. <u>No</u> mail has arrived.   _____

9. Are <u>ladies'</u> shoes on display there?   _____

10. Checkers is <u>our</u> most colorful game.   _____

11. He owns <u>twenty-two</u> rare coins.   _____

12. Does <u>this</u> art class appeal to you?   _____

13. <u>The</u> cabinet makers met in New York.   _____

14. They visited <u>their</u> old meeting place.   _____

15. <u>Father's</u> uncle once lived in a ghost town.   _____

Name_____   **NOUNS**
                                        Determiners

Date_____

Directions: Place <u>D</u> in the provided space if the underlined word serves as a
              determiner. Then circle the noun it modifies in the sentence. Place <u>N</u>
              in the space provided if the underlined word does not serve as a
              determiner.

        Example: ___D___   <u>My</u> alarm clock didn't go off.

_____   1.   <u>Those</u> book ends are made of brass.

_____   2.   Are you taking <u>those</u> with you?

_____   3.   <u>Fifty</u> will be admitted.

_____   4.   Charles earned <u>fifty</u> dollars by mowing lawns.

_____   5.   <u>Some</u> clay lay on the table.

_____   6.   We chose <u>some</u> of the latest tapes.*

_____   7.   Was <u>her</u> lecture easy to follow?

_____   8.   Go with <u>her</u>.

_____   9.   What are <u>these</u>?

_____   10. Our baker likes <u>these</u> old types of pans.

_____   11. Were there <u>fourteen</u> candles on the cake?

_____   12. My brother purchased <u>fourteen</u> of the denim shirts.*

_____   13. <u>Many</u> of the streets were flooded.

_____   14. Do you have <u>many</u> relatives in this city?

_____   15. The <u>cactus's</u> flowers were in bloom.

COMMON AND PROPER NOUNS

By definition, common nouns do not name specific persons, places, or things. Most nouns are common nouns.

By definition, proper nouns name specific persons, places, or things. Proper nouns are capitalized.

common noun: cat

proper noun: Miss Kitty

common noun: bank

proper noun: People's Trust Bank

Examples of common and proper nouns:

common noun	type (still a common noun)	proper noun
building	bank	Freestone Bank
bird	canary	Tweety Bird
horse	palomino	Trigger

Name_____   **NOUNS**
                                                            Common and Proper
Date_____

Directions: In the space provided, write a proper noun for each common noun.

    Example: person:_____George Washington_____

1.   river: _____

2.   actor: _____

3.   club: _____

4.   street: _____

5.   country: _____

6.   athlete: _____

7.   city: _____

8.   school: _____

9.   lake: _____

10.   building: _____

11.   company: _____

12.   singer: _____

13.   mountain: _____

14.   store: _____

15.   ocean: _____

Name_____

Date_____

Directions: In the space provided, write <u>C</u> if the word is a common noun and a <u>P</u> if the word is a proper noun.

1. ____ dictionary	21. ____ comedy
2. ____ Lake Mead	22. ____ Gulf of Mexico
3. ____ <u>U.S.S. Arizona</u>	23. ____ General Electric Co.
4. ____ plans	24. ____ Wayside Inn
5. ____ <u>Bible</u>	25. ____ career
6. ____ strawberries	26. ____ clerk
7. ____ spas	27. ____ Dr. Billings
8. ____ parents	28. ____ magazine
9. ____ Florida	29. ____ Camelback Mountain
10. ____ stereo	30. ____ restaurant
11. ____ Empire State Building	31. ____ United States
12. ____ Red Cross	32. ____ Disneyland
13. ____ Mason & Dixon Line	33. ____ island
14. ____ van	34. ____ Yosemite National Park
15. ____ Edgewater Church	35. ____ church
16. ____ Girl Scouts	36. ____ Meteor Crater
17. ____ roses	37. ____ zoo
18. ____ Third Avenue	38. ____ hotel
19. ____ Lamplighter Diner	39. ____ Fourth of July
20. ____ Mars	40. ____ parrot

Name_____   **NOUNS**

Date_____

Directions: Underline any noun(s) in the following sentences.

Example: Some <u>motorcycles</u> were parked in the <u>front</u>.

1.   Remove the pencils, papers, and rulers from your desk.

2.   Our total bill for the delightful lunch was twelve dollars.

3.   On the farm we saw pigs, cows, chickens, and several horses.

4.   Her last game of the season was played at a local stadium.

5.   That gold cup was given to my grandmother by some famous actress.

6.   We enjoy many freedoms such as liberty and justice.

7.   An elm tree grew in their yard for forty-seven years.

8.   Those bruises from the accident should be checked by a doctor.

9.   No grass will grow on the side of that stony hill.

10.   Your wallet, credit cards, and loose change are on the bed.

11.   During our break, Stephanie's mother brought in drinks and cookies.

12.   In Bert's report, he wrote about zoo animals.

13.   A slithering snake crawled out of those woods this morning.

14.   Were their street lights repaired after the dangerous storm?

15.   Some things, like love and truth, are not purchased with any money.

16.   A table with six chairs was delivered in several large cartons.

17.   The miners searched for gold in the hills of North Dakota.

18.   Dad's gift was a beautiful bouquet of roses, carnations, and ferns.

19.   Trucks, puzzles, and coloring books lay on the child's floor.

20.   Two classmates sent some invitations to members of their group.

SINGULAR AND PLURAL NOUNS

Singular means one.

Plural means more than one.

<u>Rule AA:</u> **The plural of most words is made by adding <u>s</u> to the singular form.**

map	dent	basket
maps	dents	baskets

<u>Rule A:</u> **When a singular word ends in <u>s</u>, <u>sh</u>, <u>ch</u>, <u>x</u>, or <u>z</u>, <u>es</u> will be added to form the plural.**

class	wish	church	box	buzz
classes	wishes	churches	boxes	buzzes

<u>Rule B:</u> **When a singular word ends in <u>ay</u>, <u>ey</u>, <u>oy</u>, or <u>uy</u>, <u>s</u> will be added to form the plural.**

bay	key	boy	guy
bays	keys	boys	guys

<u>Rule C:</u> **When a word ends in <u>consonant + y</u>, the y is changed to i, and <u>es</u> will be added to form the plural.**

baby	candy	battery	cry
babies	candies	batteries	cries

SINGULAR AND PLURAL NOUNS

Rule D: **Some words totally change in the plural form.**

man	woman	child	goose
men	women	children	geese

Use a dictionary to check the plural forms of nouns.

If the word totally changes to form the plural, the dictionary will spell out the plural.

Example: child (child) n., pl. children. 1. baby or infant
                        (pl. = plural)

Rule E: **Some words are the same in the singular and plural forms.**

sheep	deer	moose
sheep	deer	moose

Use a dictionary to check the plural forms of nouns.

If the word does not change from singular to plural, the dictionary will show it.

Example: moose (moos) n., pl. moose. 1. a large animal...
                        (pl. = plural)

Rule F: **Some words ending in f, change the f to v and add es to form the plural.**

calf	thief	leaf
calves	thieves	leaves

Use a dictionary to check the plural forms of nouns.

If the word changes f to v, the dictionary will show it.

Example: calf (kaf) , n., pl. calves. 1. a baby cow
                        (pl. = plural)

Rule G: **Some words ending in f do not change f to v. These words simply add s to form the plural.**

puff	whiff	grief
puffs	whiffs	griefs

126

SINGULAR AND PLURAL NOUNS

Rule H: **Some words ending in <u>o</u>, add <u>s</u> to form the plural.**

           Some words ending in <u>o</u>, add <u>es</u> to form the plural.

           Some words ending in <u>o</u>, add <u>s</u> or <u>es</u> to form the plural.

           <u>Use your dictionary to check for the correct plural form.</u>

           Examples: photo (fo to), n., <u>pl. tos</u>.
                                    (plural = photos)

                       hero   (hir o), n., <u>pl. heroes</u>.

                       zero   (zir o), n., <u>pl. ros, roes</u>.
                                    (plural = zeros, zeroes)

Rule I: **Some hyphenated words add <u>s</u> to the first part when forming the plural.**

           The same applies to non-hyphenated words.

           <u>Check your dictionary for the correct plural form.</u>

           Examples: sister-in-law
                                sisters-in-law

                                commander in chief
                                commanders in chief

NOTE: In a dictionary, if two plural forms are given, the first listed is preferred and should be used.

           Example: cactus: cacti, cactuses

                  <u>Cacti</u> should be used.

N O U N S
Plurals

Directions: Write the plural form in the space provided. In the space before the number, write the rule which applies.

Example: __B__ 1. monkey _____monkeys_____

_____	1.	pencil_____
_____	2.	gulf_____
_____	3.	dodo_____
_____	4.	mother-in-law_____
_____	5.	shirt_____
_____	6.	potato_____
_____	7.	mouse_____
_____	8.	toy_____
_____	9.	entry_____
_____	10.	idea_____
_____	11.	hobo_____
_____	12.	foot_____
_____	13.	life_____
_____	14.	louse_____
_____	15.	reply_____
_____	16.	customer_____
_____	17.	slush_____
_____	18.	tooth_____
_____	19.	spoof_____
_____	20.	tray_____
_____	21.	bunch_____
_____	22.	fox_____
_____	23.	century_____
_____	24.	generation_____
_____	25.	pet_____

Name_____   **NOUNS**
                                            Plurals
Date_____

Directions: Write the plural form in the space provided. In the space before the
              number, write the rule which applies.

        Example: __A A__ 1. star_____ stars_____

____   1. replay_____   ____   21. latch_____

____   2. box_____   ____   22. elk_____

____   3. symphony_____   ____   23. country_____

____   4. loaf_____   ____   24. essay_____

____   5. mantis_____   ____   25. father-in-law_____

____   6. soda_____   _____

____   7. ax_____

____   8. stereo_____

____   9. ox_____

____   10. push_____

____   11. funnel_____

____   12. rodeo_____

____   13. calf_____

____   14. honey_____

____   15. witch_____

____   16. press_____

____   17. hex_____

____   18. computer_____

____   19. trout_____

____   20. leaf_____

POSSESSIVE NOUNS

Rule A: **To form the possessive of a singular noun, add 's to the word.**

> Examples: truck + tires   man + wallet
>
>   truck's tires   man's wallet

> **The 's is added to all singular words, no matter in what letter the word ends.**
>
> Examples: waitress + apron   Jones + house
>
>   waitress's apron   Jones's house

Rule B: **To form the possessive of a plural noun that ends in s, simply add ' after the s (at the end of the word).**

> Examples: ladies + club   cats + dish
>
>   ladies' club   cats' dish
>
>   teachers + workroom
>
>   teachers' workroom

Rule C: **To form the possessive of a plural noun that does NOT end in s, add 's to the word.**

> Examples: children + playground   geese + formation
>
>   children's playground   geese's formation

Name_____   **N O U N S**
                                              Possessives
Date_____

Directions: Write the possessive noun and what it possesses in the space provided.

          Example: the club that belongs to three boys

          _____ boys' club _____

1.   stickers that belong to one child

_____

2.   a ring that belongs to a boy

_____

3.   a restroom that belongs to all of the ladies

_____

4.   a car that belongs to James

_____

5.   a game that belongs to all of the children

_____

6.   tools that belong to two carpenters

_____

7.   a whistle that belongs to Sam

_____

8.   a cup that belongs to an architect

_____

9.   a barn that is shared by all of the horses

_____

10.   a tail that a mouse has

_____

Directions: Write the possessive noun and what it possesses in the space provided.

Example: some pennies that belong to my brother

_____my brother's pennies_____

1.   prizes that belong to two contestants

_____

2.   a horse that my friend owns

_____

3.   a room that two brothers share

_____

4.   gifts that were given to Dad

_____

5.   a sandbox belonging to four children

_____

6.   a field where two deer stay

_____

7.   a toothbrush that belongs to Bess

_____

8.   an organization belonging to all of the men

_____

9.   luggage that belongs to a traveler

_____

10.   prayer that belongs to a child

_____

Name_____

Date_____

Directions: Write the possessive noun and what it possesses in the space provided.

Example: a foot belonging to an ox

_____an ox's foot_____

1.   a routine belonging to three dancers

_____

2.   some paintings belonging to a museum

_____

3.   a gift belonging to Dennis

_____

4.   a party given by five neighbors

_____

5.   a pathway for bikers

_____

6.   a desk belonging to a boss

_____

7.   the voice of an announcer

_____

8.   a luncheon attended by women

_____

9.   a convention attended by cooks

_____

10.   a store belonging to several owners

_____

Directions: Write the possessive noun and what it possesses in the space provided.

Example: an apartment shared by sisters

_____sisters' apartment_____

1.   cavities that are in the teeth

   _____

2.   dishes that my grandmother owns

   _____

3.   a business owned by two women

   _____

4.   a book belonging to that person

   _____

5.   a play area belonging to several babies

   _____

6.   an airplane owned by a company

   _____

7.   a hot air balloon owned by several couples

   _____

8.   a field belonging to one sheep

   _____

9.   a field belonging to many sheep

   _____

10.   a teacher that belongs to a class

   _____

A predicate nominative is a noun (or pronoun) that occurs after a linking verb and means the same as the subject.

Linking verbs: to feel   to become   to remain
                to taste   to seem   to appear
                to look   to sound   to stay
                to smell   to grow   to be (is, am, are, was, were, be, being, been)

                              P.N.
        Example: Marilyn <u>was</u> her best friend ~~in college~~.
                     Proof: <u>Her best friend was Marilyn.</u>

Remember: To prove the predicate nominative, invert the sentence. Begin with the word(s) after the verb, include the predicate nominative, and, then, go to the beginning of the sentence. This is called inverting the sentence.

Directions: Cross out any prepositional phrases. Underline the subject once and the verb/verb phrase twice. Label any predicate nominative-P.N. Write the proof for the predicate nominative on the line provided.

1.   Mr. Harrison is Charlie's tennis coach.

     Proof: _____

2.   Chess is their favorite pastime.

     Proof: _____

3.   Guam is a tropical island in the Pacific Ocean.

     Proof: _____

4.   Dr. Jones has been the head physician at that clinic for several years.

     Proof: _____

5.   During her stay with the Wings, buttered popcorn became her favorite food.

     Proof: _____

A predicate nominative is a noun (or pronoun) that occurs after a linking verb and means the same as the subject.

Directions: Cross out any prepositional phrases. Underline the subject once and the verb/verb phrase twice. Label any predicate nominative-P.N. Write the proof for the predicate nominative on the line provided.

1. Thomas Jefferson was the author of the Declaration of Independence.

    Proof: _____

2. A thick-bodied, gnawing rodent is a marmot.

    Proof: _____

3. During Zack's childhood, his favorite hobby was stamp collecting.

    Proof: _____

4. A partridge is a European game bird.

    Proof: _____

5. Thomas Edison was the inventor of the phonograph.

    Proof: _____

6. Jonah became the editor of a local newspaper.

    Proof: _____

7. The helpful woman with the Lewis and Clark expedition was Sacajawea.

    Proof: _____

8. The candidates for President in 1992 were Bill Clinton and George Bush.

    Proof: _____

APPOSITIVES

An appositive is a word or group of words (phrase or clause) that stands next to a noun. An appositive adds additional information.

An appositive is set off by a comma or commas.

Examples: Love Bug, <u>my pet canary</u>, is fed daily.   (phrase)

Ms. Tate, <u>the lady who is by the pool</u>, once won our local

golf tournament.   (clause)

Your bracelet is made of my favorite jewel, <u>emeralds</u>.

Dunn and Denver, <u>our goldfish</u>, eagerly gulp their food.   (phrase)

More than one appositive may appear in a sentence.

Examples: Lady Gray, <u>my horse</u>, and Duke, <u>my cousin's pony</u>, won first place ribbons at the fair.

Desserts, <u>peach cobbler and strawberry pie</u>, were served to fifty guests, <u>members of a wildlife club</u>.

Sometimes appositives are joined by a conjunction.

Examples: These televisions, <u>the color one and the portable one</u>, will be sold at an auction.

The gathering was attended by two special guests, <u>a cousin from Denmark and an uncle from France</u>.

Directions: Underline the appositive(s) in the following sentences.

Example: This flower, <u>an African daisy</u>, needs much water.

1. We visited Philadelphia, a city in Pennsylvania.
2. Popcorn, my favorite food, is prepared in many different ways.
3. Snoopy, a famous cartoon character, makes many people laugh.
4. Take my lunch, the one in the blue and orange bag.
5. Several students, Ron, Tammy, and Dirk, have been selected to go to a convention.
6. I spoke with Jacob L. Tompson, chief engineer for that company.
7. I like this portrait, the side view one, better.
8. Our meal, hot dogs and French fries, was delivered by a deli.
9. He chose his sister, Roberta Ann, as his running mate.
10. Water, a most refreshing drink, is very good for you.
11. Watch out for those golfers, those in red sweaters.
12. My father, the mayor of this town, is a great fisherman.
13. This ice cream, Parker's specialty, is extremely expensive.
14. Give this to her, the young lady in the back row.
15. Brian, their father-in-law, drives a truck for a major moving company.
16. The decorations, red and yellow streamers, had been placed on the walls before the dance had begun.
17. These glasses, some deep red goblets, belonged to Mrs. Trunman.
18. Mike, my oldest brother, has given an engagement ring to Viola, the clerk at Minton's Pharmacy.
19. Holland, a lovely country, is famous for its tulips.
20. Jim Thorpe, a famous native American, went to school in Carlisle, Pennsylvania.

Name_____

Date_____

A gerund is a word formed by adding <u>ing</u> to a verb. This is called a verbal. A gerund serves as a noun in a sentence.

Example: to skate = skating

Skating is my favorite pastime.

In this sentence, <u>skating</u> is the subject.

Example: to play = playing

We like playing in the sand.

In this sentence, <u>playing</u> is a gerund that serves as a direct object. We can delete ~~in the sand~~ as a prepositional phrase. However, we can also call <u>playing in the sand</u> a gerund phrase. A gerund phrase is made by adding a word or words to a gerund.

Directions: Cross out any prepositional phrases. Underline the subject once and the verb/verb phrase twice. Label any direct object - D.O. Then, circle any gerund.

1. Cooking is his favorite.

2. Jim loves skiing with his brother.

3. Standing in line is not fun for my grandmother.

4. Biking has become very popular.

5. Mr. and Mrs. Harris enjoy looking for sea shells at the beach.

6. During the summer, fishing is their most enjoyable pastime.

7. Exercising is great for your body.

8. Jack has started practicing for a part in the play.

A. Common or Abstract?:

Directions: Write C if the word is a concrete noun; write A if the word is an abstract noun.

1. _____ cloth
2. _____ missile
3. _____ truth
4. _____ stomach

5. _____ cheerfulness
6. _____ butter
7. _____ misunderstanding
8. _____ gorilla

9. _____ love
10. _____ slipper
11. _____ feeling
12. _____ feather

B. Common or Proper?:

Directions: Write C if the noun is common; write P if the noun is proper.

1. _____ CANYON
2. _____ CRANE
3. _____ PRATT PARK
4. _____ THOMAS
5. _____ BRYCE CANYON

6. _____ CLUB
7. _____ CONNECTICUTT RIVER
8. _____ ADAMS COUNTY FAIR
9. _____ ELEMENTARY SCHOOL
10. _____ GRANDSTAND

C. Adjective or Noun?:

Directions: Write N if the underlined word serves as a noun; write A if the underlined word serves as an adjective.

1. _____ Put this shoe <u>box</u> in the closet, please.
2. _____ A <u>box</u> lunch was served at the Valentine party.
3. _____ This <u>camera</u> cover is made of leather.
4. _____ Do you have film for the <u>camera</u>?
5. _____ Georgette has a <u>tea</u> server in her new apartment.
6. _____ Set the cup of steaming <u>tea</u> on the counter top.

140

D. **Noun or Verb?:**

Directions: Write <u>N</u> if the underlined word serves as a noun; write <u>V</u> if the
underlined word serves as a verb.

1. _____ They keep a grocery <u>list</u> on the side of the refrigerator.

2. _____ You must <u>list</u> all of your prepositions, Sherry.

3. _____ <u>Slip</u> this envelope under the back door.

4. _____ The students wrote an answer on a <u>slip</u> of paper.

5. _____ The river may <u>flood</u> during the spring.

6. _____ During the <u>flood</u>, some folks were airlifted from their homes.

E. **Plurals:**

Directions: Write the plural of each noun.

1. tooth -_____   6. library - _____

2. photo - _____   7. bunch - _____

3. wish - _____   8. prayer - _____

4. moose - _____   9. decoy - _____

5. telephone - _____   10. die - _____

F. **Possessives:**

Directions: Write the possessive noun with the the word it owns.

1. a rubber duck belonging to a toddler - _____

2. a statement belonging to the witness - _____

3. a nursery belonging to many babies - _____

4. popsicles belonging to their sister - _____

5. a room belonging to more than one fireman - _____

Name_____

Date_____

G. **Determiners and Nouns:**

Directions: Write any determiner and the noun it modifies.

1. Mark's little brother makes his own pancakes.   _____

      _____

2. This book contains many colorful pictures.   _____

      _____

3. Your tires need some air.   _____

      _____

4. A student purchased two pieces of pizza.   _____

      _____

5. Do they need these nails for their tree house?   _____

      _____

H. **Nouns Serving as Direct Objects and Indirect Objects:**

Directions: Cross out any prepositional phrases. Underline the subject
                    once and the verb/verb phrase twice.   Label any direct object-D.O.
                    Label any indirect object-I.O.

1. Miss Hanes handed the smiling bellman her luggage.

2. An excited pep squad made the team a winning banner for the pep rally.

3. The new nurse gave his patient a brochure about diabetes.

4. A seamstress sewed the bride a beautiful, satin gown with pearls and lace.

5. My grandfather tells everyone stories about his high school days in Iowa.

I. **Nouns Serving as Appositives:**
    Directions: Write the appositive in the space provided.

1. _____   Bridgette, my friend, plays the guitar.

2. _____   We called Fifi, our dog, several times.

3. _____   Sally completed her work in math, her favorite subject.

4. _____   A security officer, the gentleman in the blue uniform, checked various doors.

J. **Nouns Serving as Predicate Nominatives:**
    Directions: Cross out any prepositional phrases. Underline the subject once and the verb/verb phrase twice. Label any predicate nominative- PN. Write the proof on the line provided.

1. A neon tetra is a colorful fish.

    Proof:_____

2. The first wrestler in the meet was Adam.

    Proof:_____

3. Baby Myra was the winner of the pretty baby contest.

    Proof:_____

4. Tom Watson had become their friend after college.

    Proof:_____

K. **Noun Identification:**
    Directions: Box any noun(s).

1. Few spectators remained after the final event of the Olympics.

2. A pianist performed many famous songs for the delighted crowd.

3. My uncle and his two sons were playing tennis at a local tennis club.

4. The student, with Linda's tutoring, passed his exams with excellent grades.

5. An elephant lifted its trunk toward the tall trees and trumpeted several times.

Name_____   **CUMULATIVE REVIEW**
                                          Noun Unit
Date_____

A.   Directions: Write fifty prepositions.

1. _____   14. _____   27. _____   40. _____

2. _____   15. _____   28. _____   41. _____

3. _____   16. _____   29. _____   42. _____

4. _____   17. _____   30. _____   43. _____

5. _____   18. _____   31. _____   44. _____

6. _____   19. _____   32. _____   45. _____

7. _____   20. _____   33. _____   46. _____

8. _____   21. _____   34. _____   47. _____

9. _____   22. _____   35. _____   48. _____

10. _____   23. _____   36. _____   49. _____

11. _____   24. _____   37. _____   50. _____

12. _____   25. _____   38. _____

13. _____   26. _____   39. _____

B.   Directions: Cross out any prepositional phrases. Underline the subject once
                     and the verb/verb phrase twice.

1.   In the middle of the tournament, one chess player asked for a short break.

2.   The man with Beth and Bill has moved here from the South.

3.   During the Thanksgiving holiday, we will be going to Wisconsin.

4.   Pigeons sit above the eaves of that house on the corner.

5.   During Easter, Clyde and she will help at their church.

144

C.   Directions: Write the 23 auxiliary (helping) verbs:_____

_____

_____

D.   Write the past participle form of the following infinitives: (Write *has*, *have*, or *had* with it.)

1.   to ride - _____   11.   to teach - _____

2.   to come - _____   12.   to wear - _____

3.   to fall - _____   13.   to burst - _____

4.   to swim - _____   14.   to eat - _____

5.   to steal - _____   15.   to fly - _____

6.   to take - _____   16.   to be - _____

7.   to drink - _____   17.   to swear - _____

8.   to write - _____   18.   to bring - _____

9.   to go - _____   19.   to do - _____

10.   to buy - _____   20.   to know - _____

E.   Directions: Cross out any prepositional phrases. Underline the subject once
                        and the verb/verb phrase twice. Label any direct object-<u>D.O.</u>

1.   The speaker (rose, raised) his voice to make a point.

2.   Have you (sat, set) there for a long time?

3.   A calendar is (lying, laying) on the desk.

4.   The artist (lay, laid) two oil paintings on the oak desk.

5.   (Sit, Set) these ceramic planters out on the patio.

6.   Water had (risen, raised) in the lake after the constant rain.

F. Directions: List the 20 linking verbs (12 infinitives + 8): _____

_____

_____

G. Directions: Cross out any prepositional phrases. Underline the subject once
    and the verb twice. In the space provided, write <u>A</u> if the verb is
    action; write <u>L</u> if the verb is linking.

Remember: **Write *is*, *am*, *are*, *was*, or *were* above the verb. If the sentence makes
sense, check to see if a word in the predicate goes back to describe the
subject.**

1. _____ The toast smells burned.
2. _____ Kristina scraped the burned part from the toast.
3. _____ This stale toast tasted terrible.
4. _____ Reluctantly, Chad tasted the toast.

H. Directions: Write the contraction.

1. will not - _____   3. we are - _____   5. that is - _____

2. they are - _____   4. cannot - _____   6. was not - _____

I. Directions: Cross out any prepositional phrases. Underline the subject once and
    the verb/verb phrase twice. In the space provided, write the tense:
    *present, past, future, present perfect, past perfect, future perfect, present
    progressive, past progressive,* or *future progressive.*

1. _____ Several shoppers had stopped at a pet store.

2. _____ William's brother makes great pasta.

3. _____ The graphic artist left sketches with the owner.

4. _____ Many workers were ordering salads for lunch.

J. Directions: Circle the correct verb.

1. Several summer jobs (is, are) available.
2. Brent and Annie (ride, rides) their bikes every day.
3. One deer (limps, limp) badly.
4. Everyone of the cheerleaders (yell, yells) loudly.

146

INTERJECTIONS

Interjections are words or phrases that express strong emotion.

Interjections have an exclamation point (!) after them.

    Examples: A. **Wow!** We won!

                 B. **Good grief!** Is this my baby picture?

An interjection is a word or group of words. <u>It is not a sentence</u>. When an entire sentence reflects emotion, it is called an exclamatory sentence.

Name_____

Date_____

Directions: Underline the subject once and the verb/verb phrase twice. Circle any
              interjection(s).

      Example: **Whew**! That was a close call!

1.   Good grief! Is that picture really included in our family album?

2.   We won the tournament! Wow!

3.   Yikes! There is a snake or a turtle in the water!

4.   Oh! No! I forgot my homework!

5.   The Italian stew has too much oregano! Yuck!

6.   Boy! Are you in trouble!

7.   Yippee! A parade is coming to our town!

8.   Far out! John and I have been chosen for the debating team!

9.   No! Don't go!

10.   Someone has broken my favorite porcelain doll! Boo!

11.   Shhh! We must not wake the sleeping baby!

12.   A group of us had nearly drowned! Whew!

13.   Man! Look at those performing acrobats!

14.   Drat! Our aunt and uncle cannot take us water skiing today!

15.   Oh! Stop a minute and listen to the lovely chimes!

CONJUNCTIONS

Conjunctions are connecting words.

The most common conjunctions are: **and, but, or.**

Conjunctions connect nouns: Blueberries **and** cream taste good.

Conjunctions connect pronouns: She **or** I will go tonight.

Conjunctions connect adjectives: A blue **and** red helicopter landed.

Conjunctions connect adverbs: We wrote quickly **but** neatly.

Conjunctions connect prepositions: The ball bounced into the living room **and**
(prepositional phrases) down the hallway.

Conjunctions connect verbs: You may swim, hike, **or** rest today.

Conjunctions connect interjections: Yippee **and** yeah! We won!

Conjunctions even connect other conjunctions: Don't use but **or** and in that
sentence.

Conjunctions connect phrases: Do you like living in the woods **and**
wandering in the meadows?

Correlative Conjunctions:

Correlative conjunctions are a special type of conjunction.

    A. Correlative conjunctions occur in pairs.

    B. The most common correlative conjunctions are:

        1. **Both/And**   **Both** Ava **and** Robert are here.

        2. **Either/Or**   You may **either** wait here **or** go on alone.

        3. **Neither/Nor**   I want **neither** the blue **nor** the gray.

        4. **Not only/**   **Not only** was the dog taken to a veterinarian,

           But also   **but also** he was given a shot.

Note: There are other words that will serve as connecting words or conjunctions.

        Example: Your racing bike is faster than mine.

Name_____

Date_____

Directions: Circle any conjunction(s) in the following sentences.

Example: Jan **or** Libby won the race.

1.   We swept **and** washed the floors, **but** they were still a mess.
2.   Many trinkets **and** charms were for sale, **but** we bought none.
3.   Sit beside me **or** across the table from me.
4.   We left the skating rink, went home, **and** drank a soda.
5.   I like you, **but** I do not agree with your idea.
6.   Is your decision due tomorrow **or** the next day?
7.   Judy enjoys eating hot dogs **and** French fries **but** dislikes carrots.
8.   Will you practice your guitar now **or** wait until later?
9.   He came to the meeting **but** would not participate in discussion.
10.   Does Faith want salt **and** pepper **or** hollandaise sauce on her eggs?

Directions: Circle any conjunction(s) in the following sentences.

Example: **Neither** William **nor** my teacher arrived on time.

1.   **Either** you must finish **or** take it home with you.
2.   **Both** the men's **and** women's groups meet on Monday.
3.   The prince had **either** to choose to be king **or** to leave the kingdom.
4.   **Neither** the turnips **nor** the spinach pleased him.
5.   **Not only** had we accepted the package **but also** had paid the postage.
6.   The coach had chosen **both** the last **and** second string players.
7.   Your choice of **either** tacos **or** tostadas is a good one.
8.   **Neither** rain **nor** hail will keep us from going camping.
9.   That person was **not only** a finalist **but also** a medal winner.
10.   They have seen **both** the movie **and** the play of The Odd Couple.
11.   Someone said they had **neither** seen him **nor** knew his location.
12.   The symphony **either** must begin immediately **or** continue past midnight.

150

ADJECTIVES

There are two general types of adjectives: limiting adjectives and descriptive adjectives.

A. **Limiting Adjectives**

    1. **"Determiners"** are actually determining adjectives.

        a.   Articles: **a, an,** and **the**

        b.   Demonstratives: **this, that, those,** and **these**

        c.   Numbers

        d.   Possessives: **his, her, their, our, its, your, my**

        e.   Possessive noun (used as adjectives): <u>**Tom's**</u> car

        f.   Indefinites: **some, few, many, several, no, any** *

    2. Any of those "determiners" must appear before a noun or pronoun In order to function as an adjective. If any of the above words stand alone, they function as pronouns.

        Examples: <u>This</u> cord is frayed. (<u>This</u> is an adjective because it modifies or goes over to cord.)

                <u>This</u> must be changed. (<u>This</u> is not an adjective because there is not a noun or pronoun following it. <u>This</u> is a pronoun.)

                <u>Some</u> onions lay on the table. (<u>Some</u> is an adjective because it modifies or goes over to onions.)

                <u>Some</u> were not invited. (<u>Some</u> is not an adjective because there is not a noun or pronoun following it. <u>Some</u> is a pronoun.)

* There are others.

Directions: In the space provided, write the underlined, limiting adjective with the
noun or pronoun that it modifies.

Example: <u>My</u> belt is a leather one.   <u>My belt</u>_____

1.   <u>Some</u> practical jokes can be funny.   _____

2.   Are you in <u>his</u> jazz band?   _____

3.   We saw <u>an</u> elephant in the parade.   _____

4.   <u>No</u> cars may be parked here.   _____

5.   Did you bring <u>your</u> license?   _____

6.   <u>Few</u> earthquakes occur there.   _____

7.   Is <u>our</u> picnic basket in the jeep?   _____

8.   Naps were taken <u>several</u> times daily.   _____

9.   In fall some trees shed <u>their</u> leaves.   _____

10.   There are <u>three</u> red jackets.   _____

11.   Did Mr. Weber like <u>these</u> cards?   _____

12.   The <u>chair's</u> back is carved oak.   _____

13.   <u>That</u> pebble was collected for Tim.   _____

14.   There were <u>twenty-one</u> pink bikes.   _____

15.   <u>Sonny's</u> service station succeeded.   _____

Directions: Underline any article in the following sentences.

1. The receptionist wore an orange dress and a lavender pair of shoes to the office today.
2. The book club gave an exercise book as a free gift.
3. Going to Tahiti was an experience of a lifetime.

Directions: Underline any numbers that serve as adjectives in the following sentences.

1. We waited fifteen years to start this company.
2. Has Grace been given five or six toasters for wedding gifts?
3. Nearly forty players were aboard our flight to St. Paul.
4. One Broadway show was attended by five members of our family.
5. She saved two dollars by purchasing three products.

Directions: Underline any possessive nouns that serve as adjectives in the following sentences.

1. Jessica's new pen doesn't work properly.
2. Have you ever seen any of Tarzan's movies?
3. The birds' nest had been thrown from the tree during the storm.
4. Last night's paper reported that the women's club would meet on Tuesday.
5. Wendy's new shoes came from McMurray's Shoe Store.

Directions: Underline any adjective in the following sentences.

1. Her uncle is leaving that town in my brother's airplane.
2. Your three baseball cards are on the floor.
3. The anxious and weepy starlet had lost her emerald ring.
4. Many autograph books were passed out at a special celebration.
5. Her bright, straight teeth are beautiful.

Name_____

Date_____

Directions: Choose any demonstrative adjectives in the following sentences.

1. Those potatoes need to be peeled.

2. Did you buy that game yesterday?

3. Have you read these magazines?

4. This year has been fun.

Directions: Choose any indefinite adjectives in the following sentences.

1. Has the agent purchased many houses this year?

2. I have no coins for the machine.

3. Will we serve several vegetables for dinner?

4. Few shampoos were on sale today.

5. Do you have any money?

6. Some doughnuts will be served with breakfast.

Directions: Choose any possessive pronouns used as adjectives: <u>my</u>, <u>her</u>, <u>his</u>, <u>your</u>, <u>its</u>, <u>our</u>, <u>their</u>.

1. Your ticket is on the desk.

2. Did her pamphlet sell?

3. Some composers left their works behind.

4. What is our job?

5. Their train is leaving in an hour.

6. The monkey chased its tail and waved.

7. Do your parents know his father?

ADJECTIVES
Function?

Directions: Place <u>A</u> in the provided space if the underlined word serves as an adjective. Place <u>N</u> in the space provided if the underlined word does not serve as an adjective.

    Example: ___A___   1. <u>Some</u> shirts were on sale.

Remember: The underlined word must have a noun or pronoun closely following it in order to serve as an adjective. Be sure to cross out any prepositional phrase(s) beside an underlined word.

    Example: ___N___   2. <u>Some</u> ~~of the goats~~ stood outside the barn.

_____   1. <u>Many</u> sand buggies rode through the desert.

_____   2. <u>Many</u> had been invited.

_____   3. There were only a <u>few</u> on display.

_____   4. A <u>few</u> monkeys were swinging on the bars.

_____   5. <u>His</u> truck was in the garage.

_____   6. Is <u>his</u> broken?

_____   7. <u>Several</u> of the batteries don't work.

_____   8. I have been given <u>several</u> dollars for my birthday.

_____   9. The guides went with <u>her</u> for instruction.

_____   10. Does she know <u>her</u> coat of arms?

_____   11. Do <u>any</u> of your friends want an ice cream bar?

_____   12. Are there <u>any</u> tomatoes in the garden?

ADJECTIVES

There are two general types of adjectives: limiting adjectives and descriptive adjectives.

B. **Descriptive Adjectives**

1. **Describe**.   Examples: red, dumb, high, fine

2. Answer the question **WHAT KIND**?

3. Some descriptive adjectives end in the following suffixes:

    a. **ous**   Examples: dangerous, courageous, famous

    b. **ful**   Examples: cheerful, beautiful, sorrowful

    c. **able**   Examples: remarkable, capable, adorable

    d. **y**   Examples: silly, watery, rainy

    e. **ible**   Examples: incredible, irresistible, deductible

    f. **ive**   Examples: creative, productive, secretive

    g. **less**   Examples: priceless, penniless, sugarless

    h. **al**   Examples: special, final, postal

4. Descriptive adjectives modify or go over to a noun or pronoun.

    a.   Descriptive adjectives often come before the noun or pronoun.

        Example: **White** <u>swans</u> swam on *our* lake.

                (**White** describes swans.)
                (*Our* is a possessive going over to lake.)

        Example: *Tanya's* dog is the **playful** <u>one</u>.

                (*Tanya's* is a possessive that goes over to the noun dog.)
                (**Playful** goes over to the pronoun one.)

    b.   Descriptive adjectives sometimes come after the noun or pronoun.

        Examples: A <u>grapefruit</u>, **round** and **juicy**, was picked.

                (**Round** and **juicy** describe a grapefruit.)

                This <u>doll</u> is **old**.

                (**Old** is a predicate adjective.)

Directions: Choose any adjective(s) in the following sentences.

         Example: **Micah's black** hair is very **shiny**.

1.   Our new brick home is spacious, but the garden area is weedy.

2.   Her talkative mother uses the blue phone for endless conversations.

3.   Some slow turtles moved under a large green bush.

4.   Nancy's interesting trip to the quiet moors of the English countryside must have been fascinating.

5.   My story about our unusual vacation was funny.

6.   Their favorite guest speaker didn't require reservations.

7.   Our boys' room is an absolute mess.

8.   A few pretty fall hairdos were included in an article in this fashion magazine.

9.   Many outstanding artists held a showing at the new art gallery.

10.   Take your twenty pieces of black glass and place them in the old cedar chest.

11.   Our basic concern was for those thirty lost children.

12.   The victim, rested and thankful, returned to his suburban home.

13.   This lucky winner gave a joyful but tearful scream of complete surprise.

14.   That little, black puppy at the pet store is both loveable and affordable.

15.   My festive dessert was delicious but very sugary.

ADJECTIVES

Proper Adjectives

Proper adjectives are descriptive words derived from proper nouns. Since proper nouns are capitalized, we also capitalize proper adjectives.*

Proper Noun	**Proper Adjectives**	
Switzerland	Swiss	(cheese)
Mexico	Mexican	(culture)
China	Chinese	(food)

Sometimes the proper adjective form does <u>NOT</u> change.

Phoenix	Phoenix	(police)
Edison	Edison	(invention)
Zenith	Zenith	(television)
San Francisco	San Francisco	(trolley)
Fisher Price	Fisher Price	(game)
Mickey Mouse	Mickey Mouse	(hat)

*Check your dictionary for correct proper adjective forms.

158

Directions: Underline any proper adjective(s) in the following sentences. In the
              space provided, write the proper adjective and the noun(s) it modifies.

Example: I own an <u>american</u> flag.   _____American flag_____

1.   Have you eaten roman meal bread?   _____

2.   I like polish dancing.   _____

3.   Did Blanche order dutch tulips?   _____

4.   The japanese gardens are lovely.   _____

5.   When does the jewish new year begin?   _____

6.   The car was parked along a san diego
     freeway.   _____

7.   Several attended the european tour.   _____

8.   Those mexican jumping beans are very
     interesting.   _____

9.   The sony stereo is enjoyable.   _____

10. Jane's salad was eaten first at the
     easter dinner.   _____

11. We ate danish sweet rolls for a snack.   _____

12. The kodak pictures were returned yesterday.   _____

13. His parents met in a miami store.   _____

14. Take me to a small, swiss village.   _____

15. Doris owns a german shepherd and
     two arabian horses.   _____

                                                   _____

Name_____

Date_____

Directions: Choose any adjective(s) in the following sentences.

Example: **The black** and **white** zebra lay in **an open** meadow.

1.   The Victorian chair was covered in bright green velvet.

2.   Have the dirty bandages been removed from the large cut this morning?

3.   Her dress for the ball was glamorous and dazzling under the

shimmering, crystal lights.

4.   An old, rustic inn is their choice for a romantic vacation.

5.   Those brownies are moist and chewy, but these dozen cookies are

hard and stale.

6.   Our grandma's kitchen has pretty flowered wallpaper and an old

Franklin stove.

7.   Your neighbor's cat had seven tiny, furry kittens this morning.

8.   The new Christmas ornaments were brilliant, but our few childhood

ones seemed faded and cracked.

9.   The padding of this mattress is thicker and more absorbent for your

baby's comfort.

10.   For dinner we ate fried chicken legs, mashed potatoes, onion rings,

three bean salad, sour pickles, creamed corn, fruit pies with ice cream,

and many pitchers of iced lemon drink.

ADJECTIVES

Predicate Adjectives

1. A predicate adjective occurs <u>after the verb</u> in a statement (declarative sentence).

2. A predicate adjective always describes the subject of the sentence.

3. A sentence containing a predicate adjective must have a <u>linking verb</u>:

to feel	to become	to remain
to taste	to seem	to stay
to look	to sound	to be(is, am, are, was,
to smell	to grow	were, being, be,
to appear		been)

Remember: To check for a linking verb, try replacing the verb with a form of
<u>to be</u>. If you can do this without altering the meaning of the sentence,
the verb is linking.

Example: The milk <u>smells</u> sour.

The milk <u>is</u> sour.

4. A question (interrogative sentence) usually has the predicate adjective <u>and</u> the noun or pronoun after the verb.

Examples: <u>Are</u> your <u>eyes</u> **blue**?   <u>Does</u> the <u>cake</u> <u>seem</u> **flat**?

Suggestion: Make a question into a statement and then find the predicate adjective.

Your <u>eyes</u> <u>are</u> **blue**.   The <u>cake</u> <u>does seem</u> **flat**.

5. <u>**When you believe there is a predicate adjective in the sentence, ask yourself these three questions.**</u>

A. Is there a linking verb?
B. Does the adjective occur after the verb?
C. Does the adjective go back and describe the subject?

If the answer to all three of these questions is <u>YES</u>, you have a predicate adjective.

Name_____

Date_____

Directions: Underline the subject once and the verb/verb phrase twice. Circle any predicate adjective. Write the predicate adjective and the noun or pronoun it modifies (goes to) in the space provided.

Example: You look **tired**.   _____tired you (person)_____

1.   My bowling ball is blue.   _____

2.   Do you feel happy?   _____

3.   This book is interesting.   _____

4.   Some apples tasted tart.   _____

5.   My luggage is very old.   _____

6.   The bread became stale.   _____

7.   This lesson has been difficult.   _____

8.   A few children felt sick.   _____

9.   My answer sounded stupid.   _____

10.   Many cups were empty.   _____

11.   Those muffins smell good.   _____

12.   My feelings remain fond for you.   _____

13.   Will your hair stay short for the summer months?   _____

14.   Some dolphins were amusing.   _____

15.   That silver appears tarnished.   _____

Name_____   **ADJECTIVES**
                                        Predicate Adjectives
Date_____

Directions: Underline the subject once and the verb/verb phrase twice. Label any
               predicate adjective (P.A.). Write the predicate adjective and the noun or
               pronoun it modifies (goes to) in the space provided.

                              P.A.
               Example: The <u>music</u> <u>is</u> too loud.   ____loud music____

1.   This paper feels rough.   _____

2.   That child seems restless.   _____

3.   A crane's legs are too long.   _____

4.   The onion smelled strong.   _____

5.   A siren sounded shrill.   _____

6.   The fighter remained angry.   _____

7.   Dinner smells delicious.   _____

8.   My vegetable soup tastes spicy.   _____

9.   The contestant became excited.   _____

10.   Our mother is very intelligent.   _____

11.   Your eyes appear swollen.   _____

12.   This room is cooler.   _____

13.   We grow impatient in crowds.   _____

14.   The chocolate fudge was sticky.   _____

15.   Ted's sauce was too lemony.   _____

Directions: If the underlined word is a predicate adjective, place <u>P.A.</u> in the space provided. If the underlined word is NOT a predicate adjective, place <u>NOT</u> in the space provided.

<u>Remember:</u> When you believe there is a predicate adjective in the sentence, ask yourself these three questions:

A. Is there a linking verb?

B. Does the adjective occur after the verb (in a statement)?

C. Does the adjective go back and describe the subject?

If the answer is YES to all three questions, the word is a predicate adjective.

_____ 1. Our balloons are <u>red</u>.

_____ 2. Our car has become <u>dirty</u>.

_____ 3. We chose the <u>purple</u> toothbrush.

_____ 4. The sky grew <u>cloudy</u>.

_____ 5. These four books are <u>great</u>.

_____ 6. Their grandmother scrubbed clothes on a <u>wooden</u> scrub board.

_____ 7. That house seems <u>haunted</u>.

_____ 8. Have you painted the <u>yellow</u> house?

_____ 9. Lance tasted several types of <u>brick</u> cheese.

_____ 10. Fried shrimp tasted <u>good</u>.

_____ 11. Flowers grew <u>three</u> inches.

_____ 12. After the long night, the nurse grew very <u>weary</u>.

ADJECTIVES

Degrees of Adjectives

Adjectives often make comparisons.

    A. The **comparative form** compares **two**.

    B. The **superlative form** compares **three or more**.

Examples: This painting is **larger** than that one.

           (Comparative form - comparing two)

      Of the three, this painting is **largest**.

           (Superlative form - comparing three or more)

There are several ways to form the comparative and superlative forms:

    A. **Comparative:**

        1. Add **er** to most one-syllable adjectives.

           high/high**er**   big/bigg**er**

        2. Add **er** to many two-syllable adjectives.

           lovely/loveli**er**   happy/happi**er**

        3. Place **more** (or **less**) before many two-syllable adjectives.

           partial/**more** partial   loyal/**less** loyal

        4. **Some adjectives totally change form**.

           good/better   bad/worse

    B. **Superlative:**

        1. Add **est** to most one-syllable adjectives.

           high/high**est**   big/bigg**est**

        2. Add **est** to many two-syllable adjectives.

           lovely/loveli**est**   happy/happi**est**

ADJECTIVES

Degrees of Adjectives

B. **Superlative (cont.)**

   3. Place **most** (or **least**) before many two-syllable adjectives.

   partial/**most** partial   loyal/**least** loyal

   Suggestion: Use your dictionary to determine if <u>est</u> should be added to the adjective. If the dictionary does NOT give the <u>est</u> form, use <u>most</u> (or <u>least</u>) before the adjective.

   4. Place **most** (or **least**) before three-syllable adjectives.

   wonderful/**most** wonderful

   beautiful/**most** beautiful

   expensive/**least** expensive

   5. **Some adjectives totally change form.**

   good/best   bad/worst

Name_____

Date_____

Directions: Write the required comparative or superlative form of the given adjective in the space provided.

Example: superlative form of creative

_____most creative_____

1. comparative form of red

_____

2. superlative form of special

_____

3. superlative form of sincere

_____

4. comparative form of good

_____

5. comparative form of fast

_____

6. comparative form of festive

_____

7. superlative form of dirty

_____

8. superlative form of marvelous

_____

9. comparative form of generous

_____

10. superlative form of bad

_____

Name_____

Date_____

Directions: Choose the correct adjective in each sentence.

Example: Rene is the (faster, **fastest**) runner in our class.

1.   This sandwich is (more delicious, most delicious) than that one.

2.   Of the triplets, Peter is (smaller, smallest).

3.   Olivia's hair is (curlier, curliest) than when she was a baby.

4.   This is the (more dangerous, most dangerous) road I have ever driven on.

5.   Lois is a (gooder, better) mechanic than I.

6.   That hill is the (taller, tallest) one of the three.

7.   This is the (more fantastic, most fantastic) book of the twenty that I have read this year.

8.   Of all the circus acts, the dog jumping was (sillier, silliest).

9.   Both rings are lovely, but I think the larger one is (more attractive, most attractive).

10.   My new car is (more powerful, most powerful) than my old one.

11.   She is the (luckier, luckiest) person I know.

12.   I think that this puppy is the (more loveable, most loveable) one of the entire litter.

13.   The mush ball is (softer, softest) than the large, black ball.

14.   This is the (baddest, worst) show I have ever seen.

15.   Which one of the twins is (more sensitive, most sensitive)?

Directions: Choose the correct adjective form in each sentence.

1.   This day is (funner, more fun) than yesterday.

2.   Of the two paintings, I like this one (better, best).

3.   Which train, the Slimton Express or the Apache Racer, is (faster, fastest)?

4.   Our new house is (larger, largest) than our old one.

5.   Of our three dogs, that one is (more gentle, most gentle).

6.   I think that red is (brighter, brightest) of the colors in a rainbow.

7.   This math problem is (more difficult, most difficult) than the one before it.

8.   You are the (nicer, nicest) person I know.

9.   Are the bananas or the grapes (tastier, tastiest)?

10.   This is the (more interesting, most interesting) flower in the exotic flower show.

11.   Chuck is (livelier, liveliest) of the four brothers.

12.   Your photograph looks (more natural, most natural) than mine.

13.   Of all the pancakes, this blueberry one is (rounder, roundest).

14.   Your hair is (curlier, curliest) than Krista's.

15.   This is the (taller, tallest) building in the city.

Name_____

Date_____

A. Limiting Adjectives:

Directions: Fill in the blank.

1. The three limiting adjectives that are also called articles are _____, _____, and _____.

2. Four demonstrative words that may serve as limiting adjectives are _____, _____, _____, and _____.

3. The possessive pronouns that may serve as limiting adjectives are _____, _____, _____, _____, _____, _____, and _____.

4. Four examples of indefinites that may serve as limiting adjectives are _____, _____, _____, and _____.

5. Write an example showing a number used as a limiting adjective:_____.

6. Write an example showing a possessive noun serving as a limiting adjective: _____

_____

B. Limiting Adjective or Pronoun?

Directions: Write <u>A</u> in the space provided if the boldfaced word serves as an adjective; write <u>P</u> if the boldfaced word serves as a pronoun (stands alone). After the sentence, write the limiting adjective and the noun it modifies. (The line after any sentence marked <u>P</u> will be blank .)

Example: __A__   **My** room is clean.   ____My room_____

__P__   I like **that**!   _____

1. _____   They spent **five** dollars for a ticket.   _____
2. _____   **Five** must agree to help.   _____
3. _____   **Several** watched shoppers pass by.   _____
4. _____   **Several** babies began to cry.   _____
5. _____   I would like **those** with bows.   _____
6. _____   Please hand me **those** magazines.   _____

Date_____

C. **Descriptive Adjectives:**
   Directions: Write three descriptive adjectives for each noun.

1. ball - _____

2. room - _____

3. woman - _____

4. day - _____

D. **Predicate Adjectives:**
   Directions: Cross out any prepositional phrases. Underline the subject once
              and the verb/verb phrase twice. Label any predicate adjective-P.A.
              On the line, write the predicate adjective and the noun it modifies.

1. A few winter storms had been fierce.   _____

2. A customer seemed angry about the service.   _____

3. That fire drill bell sounds shrill.   _____

4. The young lady is excited about her new job.   _____

5. At the end of the day, he grows very weary.   _____

E. **Proper Adjectives:**
   Directions: Underline any proper adjective and capitalize it. In the space
              provided, write the proper adjective and the noun it modifies.

1. A spanish village is very charming. _____

2. John was born in a chicago suburb. _____

3. Do you have a sears catalog?   _____

4. Kendra likes swedish meatballs.   _____

5. Have you seen a franklin stove?   _____

F. **Degrees:**
    Directions: Circle the correct adjective form.

1. The red petunia is (healthier, healthiest) than the pink one.

2. This small yellow car is the (cheaper, cheapest) one on the entire lot.

3. The polka is a (livelier, liveliest) dance than the rumba.

4. Of all the days last week, Saturday was the (gloomier, gloomiest).

5. This glass vase looks (more fragile, most fragile) than the ceramic one.

6. Mrs. Jones's new car is (longer, longest) than her old one.

7. That man is (friendliest, friendlier) in the neighborhood.

8. Julio is the (more creative, most creative) triplet.

G. **Adjective Identification:**
    Directions: Circle any adjectives.

**Suggestion: First, look for limiting adjective(s). Then, reread the
                  sentence and circle any adjective(s) that describe.**

1. Molly's dress had a plain top and a lovely flowered skirt.

2. The dental technician gave the happy child a funny sticker and a sugarless candy.

3. Several cows grazed in the lush green meadow behind a large barn.

4. His recent speech discussed the city's plan for crime control.

5. Gloria spoke to her younger brother about the three snakes in his room.

6. An argument between the two angry boys was settled by their wise mother.

7. Many pioneers traveled by covered wagon on these marked trails.

A. Directions: Cross out any prepositional phrases. Underline the subject once
                 and the verb/verb phrase twice. Label any predicate nominative-<u>PN</u>
                 Write the proof in the space provided.

1. The admission price was one dollar for children under twelve.

    Proof: _____

2. Janice's best friend is my sister.

    Proof: _____

3. Daffodils have become Miss Hine's favorite flowers.

    Proof: _____

B. Directions: Write <u>N</u> if the boldfaced word serves as a noun; write <u>V</u> if the boldfaced
                 word serves as a verb.

1. _____ Does the toddler **dress** himself?

2. _____ The checkered **dress** has a red scarf.

3. _____ Farmer Mills **plows** his field each spring.

4. _____ Those antique **plows** are made of iron.

C. Directions: Write the past participle form.

1. to teach - _____   6. to be - _____

2. to swim - _____   7. to ride - _____

3. to burst - _____   8. to bring - _____

4. to beat - _____   9. to fly - _____

5. to freeze - _____   10. to spring - _____

D. Directions: Write the possessive:

1. a comb belonging to Mary: _____

2. streets in a city: _____

3. a trail for motor scooters: _____

4. a sandbox belonging to more than one child: _____

E. Directions: Write the contraction:

1. will not - _____   3. I am - _____   5. does not - _____

2. I would - _____   4. are not - _____   6. we are - _____

F. Directions: Cross out any prepositional phrases. Underline the subject once and
the verb/verb phrase twice. Write <u>A</u> if the boldfaced verb serves as an
action verb; write <u>L</u> if the boldfaced verb serves as a linking verb.

Suggestion: **To help determine if the verb is linking, place *is, am, are, was,* or *were*
above each verb.**

1. _____   He always **tastes** his vegetables first.

2. _____   Please **remain** by the doors.

3. _____   Fertilizer has been **placed** on the plants.

4. _____   Her eyes **grow** irritated from pollen in the air.

G. Directions: Write the plural of the following nouns. (Use a dictionary if necessary.)

1. spoonful - _____   6. father-in-law - _____

2. dairy - _____   7. mouse - _____

3. hero - _____   8. leaf - _____

4. elk - _____   9. spoof - _____

5. flash - _____   10. iris - _____

174

H. Directions: Cross out any prepositional phrases. Underline the subject once
and the verb/verb phrase.

1. The baby's rattle is (lying, laying) beside the crib.

2. Bob (lay, laid) his head on a pillow.

3. (Rise, Raise) for the singing of "The Star-Spangled Banner".

4. The fishermen are (sitting, setting) their tackle along the river's banks.

5. Have you ever (set, sat) among the pigeons in the park?

I. Directions: Write A if the boldfaced word serves as a limiting adjective and *No*
if the boldfaced word does not serve as a limiting adjective.

1. _____ **Several** have been spotted near the woods.

2. _____ **Several** advertisements appeared in the newspaper.

3. _____ You must try **those** sometime.

4. _____ Have you ever tried **those** salads in a bag?

5. _____ Harriet has been given **twenty** bulbs to plant.

6. _____ **Our** minister is also an author.

7. _____ Is **this** yours?

J. Directions: Write any limiting adjective and the noun it modifies (goes to) in the
space provided.

1. _____ Their duties include raising money for zoos.

2. _____ Were you planning on making some fudge?

3. _____ Last June, Karen's mother was ill.

4. _____ A final game was played on Saturday.

K. Directions: Write C if the word is concrete; write A if the word is abstract.

1. ____ glory   2. ____ sorrow   3. ____ field   4. ____ pole   5. ____ fun

L. Directions: Circle any adjectives.

Suggestion: First, identify limiting adjectives.   Then, look for descriptive adjectives.

1. An eager girl jumped up and down with great enthusiasm.

2. Few deer live in the wooded area near that frozen lake.

3. Those are his favorite chocolate chip cookies.

4. Our front yard has several trees and a bed of tiny purple flowers.

5. Small brushes and three gallons of dark latex paint had been placed on the bench of a house painter.

M. Directions: Go back to part L. Write any noun(s) on the line provided.

Suggestion: Use limiting and descriptive adjectives to help locate nouns.

Sentence 1: _____

Sentence 2: _____

Sentence 3: _____

Sentence 4: _____

Sentence 5: _____

N. Directions: Cross out any prepositional phrases. Underline the subject once and the verb/verb phrase twice. In the space provided, write the tense: *present, past, future, present perfect, past perfect, future perfect, present progressive, past progressive,* or *future progressive.*

1. _____   The mechanic has repaired the motorcycle.

2. _____   Peter usually sleeps under a fan.

3. _____   During a break, Kay went outside for fresh air.

4. _____   A damp cloth is lying by the washed car.

5. _____   I shall put this into my pocket.

O. Directions: Write the correct form.

1. comparative of strong: _____

2. superlative of fine: _____

3. comparative of horrible: _____

4. comparative of good: _____

5. superlative of fantastic: _____

P. Directions: Underline the entire noun appositive (phrase) in each sentence.
    Remember: A phrase is a group of words.

1. We called to Corky, our dog.

2. Her friends, Martin and Beth, will be going to the fair.

3. Would you like this dessert, a hot fudge sundae?

4. The winner, the man in the blue sweater, smiled shyly.

Q. Directions: Circle the verb that agrees with the subject.

1. Several plumbers (is, are) planning to work on that building.

2. One of the twirlers (bring, brings) her own music.

3. Mrs. Cole and her daughter (buy, buys) generic brands.

4. Mom and my brother (go, goes) hiking often.

5. Everyone of the boys (was, were) attentive.

R. Fill in the blank.

1. **A stomata is an opening in a plant.** The word, *plant*, is a noun. It serves as the
    _____ of the preposition.

2. **His uncle is an Alaskan businessman.**   The word, *Alaskan*, is what type of an
    adjective? _____

3. **You might be elected the next treasurer of the club.** The verb phrase of this
    sentence is _____. The main verb is _____.

4. **That bat is very old.** Is the word, *old*, a predicate nominative or a predicate
    adjective? _____

5. An example of an interjection is _____.

6. What are the three coordinating conjunctions? _____, _____, _____.

TYPES OF SENTENCES

There are four types of sentences:

Declarative (statement):	That barn is rustic.
Interrogative (question):	Where's the mop?
Imperative (command):	Take this.
Exclamatory (strong feeling):	This tastes terrible!

Both the **declarative** and the **imperative** sentence end with a period.

Declarative:	The high chair is yellow.
Imperative:	Please pass the butter.

An **interrogative** sentence ends with a question mark.

Interrogative:	How old are these brass beds?

An **exclamatory** sentence ends with an exclamation mark.

Exclamatory:	What a good time we had!

Note: In an interrogative sentence, the entire clause is a question.

Example: Who has decided to be chairperson of this committee?

A sentence will be **declarative**, and not interrogative, even if part of the sentence infers a question.

Examples: Mother asked if we could stay longer.

Jacob wants to know how long to cook a hard-boiled egg.

178

Name_____

Date_____

Directions: Write the sentence type: imperative, declarative, interrogative, or exclamatory.

1. _____ What did you do last night?

2. _____ Our pencil sharpener is broken.

3. _____ I want off!

4. _____ Sit up, please.

5. _____ Has the pest control person sprayed this house?

6. _____ I think that our exercise machine needs heavier weights.

7. _____ Have you seen Gone with the Wind?

8. _____ Be quiet.

9. _____ Yippee! They won the championship!

10. _____ Shadows in the room made the atmosphere very scary.

11. _____ I lost my wallet!

12. _____ Those letters were addressed to a king.

13. _____ When are the flying instructions offered?

14. _____ Brandon wants to know how you're feeling.

15. _____ How lovely you look, Miss Jones!

16. _____ Dad asked us to take out our trash.

Name_____

Date_____

Directions: Write the sentence type: imperative, declarative, interrogative, or exclamatory. **Include end punctuation.**

1. _____ Hurrah!   I made it

2. _____ Fill out this card

3. _____ Does stress actually cause cavities

4. _____ The public library opens at ten o'clock

5. _____ How terrific you look in red

6. _____ Yikes!   I knew this would happen

7. _____ Do you have any idea what this item costs

8. _____ Your sister asked us to visit

9. _____ His turn is next

10. _____ Sharon asks strange questions in science class

11. _____ Move to the end of the line

12. _____ May James and I discuss this matter with you in your office

13. _____ A small brown dog chased some sheep

14. _____ Melinda wants to know if she may go for pizza with us

15. _____ Please park your car over there

16. _____ The child often asks questions when his mother is reading to him

SENTENCES
FRAGMENTS
RUN-ONS

RUN-ONS:

A. **A run-on may consist of two independent clauses run together.**

S   V   S V

This <u>cookie</u> <u>tastes</u> good <u>I</u> <u>like</u> that one better.

B. **A run-on may consist of two independent clauses joined by a comma.**

S V   S   V

My <u>friend</u> <u>is</u> Amie, <u>she</u> <u>lives</u> next door.

C. **A run-on may consist of a group of sentences combined with too many conjunctions.**

We went to the store <u>and</u> we bought some bananas <u>and</u> we talked to our neighbor who just returned from his vacation <u>but</u> we still had time to return home <u>and</u> make our favorite cake <u>and</u> then we went jogging.

D. **A run-on may consist of a group of sentences combined with commas.**

With winter approaching, I become more anxious about skiing, sledding is going to be fun too, I mostly like to ice skate on a frozen lake.

CORRECTING RUN-ONS:

<u>In a run-on containing two independent clauses, there are three methods of correction.</u>

1. **Use a period between the independent clauses.**

    This cookie tastes good. I like that one better.

2. **Use a semicolon between the independent clauses.**

    This cookie tastes good; I like that one better.

3. **Use a comma and an appropriate conjunction between the independent clauses.**

    This cookie tastes good, but I like that one better.

In addition, one of the independent clauses may be changed to a dependent clause.

Although this cookie tastes good, I like that one better.

SENTENCES
FRAGMENTS
RUN-ONS

SENTENCES:

Clauses:

A.   An independent clause contains a subject and verb.
An independent clause expresses a complete thought.
An independent clause can stand alone as a sentence.

    Independent Clause: I <u>have</u> a record player.

B.   A dependent clause contains subject and verb.
A dependent clause does not express a complete thought.
A dependent clause cannot stand alone as a sentence.
A dependent clause without an independent clause is a <u>fragment</u>.

    Dependent Clause: When <u>you</u> <u>return</u> from the game.

Fragments:

A.   An unattached dependent clause is a fragment.

    Whenever <u>I</u> <u>am</u> lonely.

B.   A fragment sometimes contains a subject <u>or</u> verb.

    The <u>conductor</u> during the performance.
    <u>Drew</u> several pictures for us.

C.   A fragment may contain neither subject nor verb.

    Tomorrow.
    In the bottom drawer.
    From this point to that one.

D.   A command is NOT a fragment. Some commands may be only one word, but the subject is (<u>You</u>) meaning *You Understood.*

    (<u>You</u>)   <u>Go</u>!
    (<u>You</u>)   <u>Do</u> it now.

Name_____

Date_____

Directions: In the space provided, write <u>S</u> for sentence, <u>F</u> for fragment, and <u>R-O</u> for run-on.

Example: ___R-O___ The milk is old, it's sour.

_____ 1. Please call me later.

_____ 2. Fine.

_____ 3. Who has won?

_____ 4. Disturbing the peace.

_____ 5. The plant is wilting, water it.

_____ 6. A soccer ball was kicked to the far end of the field.

_____ 7. My firm answer is no, you may not go.

_____ 8. Copying the lesson from the book.

_____ 9. Matt up to me suspiciously.

_____ 10. A snake slithered under a rock.

_____ 11. My opinion is that you should keep the kitten, it definitely needs good care and you can give him a good home.

_____ 12. Our clothes were packed and ready for our trip.

_____ 13. At the end of the story.

_____ 14. Be prepared to make sudden stops on this road.

_____ 15. When Ann was little, she dreamed of becoming a doctor.

Directions: In the space provided, write S for sentence, F for fragment, and
R-O for run-on.

Example: __F__   Down the street.

_____ 1. Her jewelry had been appraised and insured.

_____ 2. After your fine presentation.

_____ 3. Mother drove the car Dad flew.

_____ 4. Talking on the telephone at the end of the day.

_____ 5. Can the roofer repair the damage?

_____ 6. Unless Mrs. Farmington calls.

_____ 7. Go!

_____ 8. Look around, plan on buying at least one gift.

_____ 9. This room is too dark and crowded.

_____ 10. After beginning the day in a wonderful mood, he was rushed
to the hospital for stitches in his left foot which he received when
he broke a glass and stepped on a small fragment, and then the
day became worse.

_____ 11. This airplane is old.

_____ 12. Walked and ran in his sleep last night.

_____ 13. A computer class is offered, I'm taking it.

_____ 14. If you need a ride.

_____ 15. Send me your new address.

PHRASE OR CLAUSE?

PHRASE: **A phrase does not contain a subject and verb.**

        Examples: down the street

                     living in Atlanta

CLAUSE: **A clause contains a subject and a verb.**

A. A **dependent clause** contains a subject **and** verb, but it does not express a complete thought. A dependent clause cannot stand alone as a sentence.

        Examples: When <u>Todd was</u> little

                         If <u>you were</u> right

                         Although <u>school had ended</u>

                         Whenever <u>I hurry</u> ~~through dinner~~ and <u>eat</u> fast

B. An **independent clause** contains subject **and** verb and expresses a complete thought. An independent clause can stand alone as a sentence.

        Examples: The air <u>deodorizer is gone</u>.

                         The <u>ten</u> of hearts <u>is missing</u> from this deck.

                         The <u>ten</u> ~~of hearts~~ <u>is missing</u> ~~from this deck~~.

                         Both the <u>man</u> and his <u>wife signed</u> several legal papers.

Directions: Write <u>C</u> on the line if the group of words is a clause.   Write <u>P</u> on the line
if the group of words is a phrase.

   Suggestion: Cross out any prepositional phrases. Underline the subject
once and the verb/verb phrase twice. If the sentence contains
both a subject and a verb, it is a clause.

Example: ___C___   The <u>fork</u> <u>was</u> ~~on the floor~~.

_____   1.   Without supper.

_____   2.   Danced in the breeze.

_____   3.   Our oven door is broken.

_____   4.   After my homework was completed.

_____   5.   Participating in a game.

_____   6.   The man in the park.

_____   7.   Even though I agreed.

_____   8.   Hurried down the lane.

_____   9.   Leaves have fallen from the trees.

_____   10.   Hanging on the wall over a fireplace.

_____   11.   No one emptied the trash.

_____   12.   Those large white eggs on the table.

_____   13.   Our basement is a storage area.

_____   14.   If I could skate faster.

_____   15.   Regardless of the telephone's dial tone.

Name_____

Date_____

Directions: Write DC on the line if the clause is a dependent clause.   Write IC
on the line if the clause is an independent clause.

Example: ___IC___   The miniature horses are as small as
dogs.

_____   1. That store opens at nine o'clock.

_____   2. Unless you plan on leaving.

_____   3. Whatever the circumstances are.

_____   4. Bottled water was delivered to their door.

_____   5. Go away.

_____   6. If our ship arrives early.

_____   7. Whenever we finish this task.

_____   8. During the power failure, our lights went out.

_____   9. Stop.

_____   10. Although the dam broke.

_____   11. Laughing and splashing, the two boys played in the pool.

_____   12. After I run these errands.

_____   13. Mr. Dobbins loves chocolate chip cookies.

_____   14. From the time I was three years old.

_____   15. Harriet vowed never to do that again.

*Remember that You, (called *you understood*), is often the subject of an imperative
sentence (command).

ADVERBS

ADVERBS TELL HOW, WHERE, WHEN, AND TO WHAT EXTENT (HOW MUCH).

Adverbs that tell HOW:

An adverb that tells **how** usually modifies or goes back to the verb/verb phrase.

Example: The <u>child</u> <u>speaks</u> clearly. (*Clearly* tells **how** the child speaks.)

Example: Quickly he <u>fell</u> ~~to the ground~~. (*Quickly* tells **how** he fell.)

Most adverbs that tell *HOW* end in *ly*.

Name_____   **ADVERBS**
                                                   How?
Date_____

Directions: Cross out any prepositional phrases. Underline the subject once and the
              verb/verb phrase twice. Label any adverb (ADV.) that tells **HOW**. In the
              space provided, explain the use of the adverb in the sentence.
                              ADV.
      Example: Marta slowly <u>explained</u> ~~about the trip to Alaska~~.
                   _____Slowly tells HOW Marta explained._____

1.   The crowd cheered happily for their team.

      _____

2.   Mary searched hurriedly through the desk drawers.

      _____

3.   Carefully the packers arranged glassware in strong boxes.

      _____

4.   A typist quickly typed an office memo for me.

      _____

5.   Bart and Melody ran fast in the fifty yard dash.

      _____

6.   That dog under the table does not feel well in this heat.

      _____

7.   He sings weirdly in the shower.

      _____

8.   Carelessly the car slid around the corner.

      _____

9.   The child was dreadfully frightened by the movie.

      _____

10.   Do you work hard on your lessons?

      _____

Directions: Underline the correct answer in the following sentences.

Example: The player ran (quick, <u>quickly</u>) to the end of the line.

1.   This is an (easy, easily) test.

2.   I can do that (easy, easily).

3.   Penguins are (slow, slowly) runners.

4.   They run (slow, slowly).

5.   Some people drive (crazy, crazily) when it rains.

6.   Does anyone think that my idea is a (crazy, crazily) one?

7.   This truck makes (sudden, suddenly) stops.

8.   It often stops (sudden, suddenly).

9.   I go swimming quite (frequent, frequently).

10.   I am a (frequent, frequently) visitor to the public pool.

11.   That is an (unkind, unkindly) thing to say.

12.   The angry person spoke (unkind, unkindly) to me.

13.   You did that (careless, carelessly).

14.   The riders went on a (peaceful, peacefully) trip in the mountains.

15.   The toddler slept so (peaceful, peacefully).

ADVERBS

Good or Well?

A. **Good is an adjective.**

They are ____**good**____ singers.

The forms of **good** are: **good**, **better**, and **best**.

They are **good** singers.

We are **better** singers than they.

Tracy is the **best** singer in the choir.

Because **good** is always an adjective, **good** will describe a noun or pronoun.

B. **Well is an adverb.**

They sing ___**well**___. (**Well** tells **HOW** they sing.)

The forms of **well** are: **well**, **better**, **best**.

They sing **well**.

We sing **better** than they.

Tracy sings **best** in our choir.

NOTE: **Well** must be used to explain **how** one does something.
Action verbs require **well** if an explanation of **how** is involved.

Examples: I swim **well**.

I play basketball **well**.

191

Directions: Fill in the blank with **good** or **well**.

Example: I am a _____good_____ ceramist.

1.   Fred plays the violin very _____.

2.   Marta is a _____engineer.

3.   _____ scissors are hard to find.

4.   Do you write _____?

5.   The ringmaster at the circus did his job _____.

6.   Are you feeling _____today?

7.   Be a _____listener.

8.   Those windows were not washed _____.

9.   Contractors worked together _____ to build that house.

10.   You did a _____ job.

11.   They were praised for their _____behavior.

12.   They behaved _____.

13.   I like my steaks cooked _____.

14.   Has your friend read two _____ books lately?

15.   Wow! You do that so _____!

192

ADVERBS

<u>**Adverbs that tell WHERE:**</u>

An adverb that tells **where** usually modifies or goes over to the verb/verb phrase.

Example: He <u>looked</u> up. (Up tells where he looked.)

There are some words that can be either a preposition **OR** an adverb. Some examples are:

IN	**OUT**
INSIDE	**OUTSIDE**
AROUND	**NEAR**
UP	**DOWN**

A.   If the word has an object (noun or pronoun), the word serves as a preposition.

Examples: <u>Dad</u> <u>fell</u> down. (<u>Down</u> is an adverb; there is no noun or pronoun following it.)

<u>Dad</u> <u>fell</u> ~~down the steps~~.   (<u>Down</u> is a preposition.)
(<u>Down the steps</u> is a prepositional phrase.

Directions: Cross out any prepositional phrases. Underline the subject once and the
              verb/verb phrase twice. Label any adverb (ADV.) that tells **WHERE**. In
              the space provided, explain the use of the adverb(s) in the sentence.

                              ADV.
         Example: We went there after school.
                          There tells WHERE we went.

1.   Have you gone anywhere in a hurry?

     _____

2.   I am going home in an hour.

     _____

3.   Marcia came in and sat down.

     _____

4.   They looked up in the sky.

     _____

5.   The boat floated downstream.

     _____

6.   You may stay there for the night.

     _____

7.   Do you live far?

     _____

8.   Somewhere my friend hid my comb.

     _____

ADVERBS

Adverbs that tell WHEN:

An adverb that tells **when** usually modifies or goes back to the verb/verb phrase.

Examples: <u>John</u> <u>left</u> early.   (*Early* tells **when** John left.)

Tonight <u>we</u> <u>will eat</u> ~~at a restaurant~~. (*Tonight* tells **when** we will eat.)

<u>You</u> <u>may go</u> later.   (*Later* tells **when** you may go.)

The <u>clerk</u> <u>was paid</u> hourly. (*Hourly* tells **when** the clerk was paid.)

Directions: Cross out any prepositional phrases. Underline the subject once and the
               verb/verb phrase twice. Label any adverb (ADV.) that tells **WHEN**. In
               the space provided, explain the use of the adverb(s) in the sentence.

                                    ADV.
    Example: We will finish the task tonight ~~after dinner~~.
                ____Tonight tells WHEN we will finish the task._____

1.   Yesterday we went to the beach with my cousin.

      _____

2.   The circus is coming to town soon.

      _____

3.   That person arrives late for every meeting.

      _____

4.   Mother purchased special pens for us today.

      _____

5.   Yearly the broker sends a stock report to his customers.

      _____

6.   I never knew about the proposed freeway.

      _____

7.   Is everyone leaving now?

      _____

8.   Will the bus be transporting early in the morning?

      _____

9.   They had been on a television show before.

      _____

10.   Tomorrow the carpenters will build a patio in our yard.

      _____

ADVERBS

Adverbs that tell TO WHAT EXTENT:

An adverb that tells **to what extent (how much)** usually modifies or goes over to an adjective or another adverb.

                                      ADJ.
    Example: The <u>rug</u> <u>is</u> **extremely** dirty.

                  (*Extremely* tells **to what extent** the rug is dirty.)
                                        ADV.
    Example: The mountain <u>climbers</u> <u>go</u> **very** slowly.

                  (*Very* tells **to what extent** the climbers go slowly.)

You need to memorize and learn the following list. These words are adverbs.

not*	**quite**	**somewhat**
so	**rather**	
very	**too**	

Occasionally **<u>so</u>, <u>very</u>, <u>too</u>, <u>rather</u>,** and **<u>quite</u>** will be within a prepositional phrase.

Cross out the prepositional phrase <u>and</u> circle the adverb.

    Example: <u>We</u> <u>went</u> ~~into a~~ **rather** ~~large estate.~~

Occasionally an adverb that tells **TO WHAT EXTENT** will modify or go to a verb.

    Example: <u>I</u> <u>would</u> **rather** <u>go</u> to the store.

                  (*Rather* tells **to what extent** I would go.)

OTHER ADVERBS THAT TELL **TO WHAT EXTENT** USUALLY END IN **<u>LY</u>**.

*<u>not</u> = <u>n't</u>.   Circle the <u>n't</u> as the ADVERB.

ADVERBS
To What Extent?

Directions: Underline any adverb(s) that tell **TO WHAT EXTENT**. Label any
other adverbs <u>ADV</u>.

                                                    ADV.
          Example: I run <u>extremely</u> slowly.

1.   The taxi arrived quite late.

2.   I did the assignment rather carefully.

3.   Often you are so hungry.

4.   Our pockets were absolutely empty.

5.   Today you look really tired.

6.   A supersonic jet flies very fast.

7.   That outfit will be too wrinkled for the banquet tonight.

8.   Our heifer is unusually thirsty lately.

9.   The lake is quite calm.

10.   Bart walked with his very glamorous grandmother.

11.   The repairman worked extremely hard yesterday.

12.   Mother and I worked well together.

13.   They arrived at the meeting too early.

14.   Aunt Lisa built a rather lovely home here.

15.   We searched the house rather frantically for the lost credit card.

ADVERBS

Adverb or Preposition?

Here is a list of words that can serve either as a preposition **OR** an adverb that tells **WHERE**:

above	up
across	in
after	out
around	inside
before	outside
down	over

<u>Any word on the preposition list that does not have a noun or pronoun following it will be an adverb.</u>

      Example: I fell ~~down the stairs~~.   (<u>Down the stairs</u> is a prepositional phrase.)

                     I fell down.   (<u>Down</u> is an adverb; there is no noun or pronoun following down.)

Cross out prepositional phrases in any sentence. Often an adverb will be beside a prepositional phrase.

      Example: The guard entered in through the security door.

      Wrong: The <u>guard</u> <u>entered</u> ~~in through the security door~~.

      Right: The <u>guard</u> <u>entered</u> in ~~through the security door~~.

                                (<u>In</u> is an adverb telling where.)

Remember: A prepositional phrase begins with a single preposition.

      Example: <u>May</u> <u>you</u> <u>come</u> over ~~to my house~~?

                      (<u>Over</u> is an adverb telling where.)

Name_____

Date_____

Directions: Place a <u>P</u> (Preposition) or <u>A</u> (Adverb) in the space provided. Be sure
to think carefully about the underlined word.

Example: __P__   The lizard crawled <u>over</u> the mound of dirt.

_____   1.   The portrait fell <u>down</u>.

_____   2.   Someone fell <u>down</u> the steps.

_____   3.   He tripped <u>over</u> the chair.

_____   4.   A dried flower arrangement fell <u>over</u> in the wind.

_____   5.   Don't jump <u>off</u> now!

_____   6.   The one year old jumped <u>off</u> the diving board.

_____   7.   <u>Before</u> lunch we shopped at a new mall.

_____   8.   Have you tried this product <u>before</u>?

_____   9.   Do you live <u>near</u> to me?

_____   10.   The old miner lived <u>near</u> the train station.

_____   11.   Go <u>up</u> the escalator and turn left.

_____   12.   Tiles in our bathroom came <u>up</u>.

_____   13.   We will not go <u>outside</u> today.

_____   14.   <u>Outside</u> the barn is an ancient tractor.

_____   15.   Come <u>in</u> please.

_____   16.   <u>In</u> the middle of the night there was a storm.

Name_____   **ADVERBS**

Date_____

Directions: Circle any adverb(s) in the following sentences.

1.   Turn the pages slowly.

2.   Now you may leave.

3.   The steeple is very tall.

4.   The jockey rode well.

5.   Today my sister broke her ankle.

6.   Go away.

7.   Stand up.

8.   Are we going anywhere?

9.   These steaks are so tender.

10.   Do not leave yet.

11.   My boss pays me hourly.

12.   Sooner or later you must know the truth.

13.   First you must turn right at Darnmon Street.

14.   Then take a bus downtown.

15.   Your feelings are hurt so easily.

16.   There are not any coins in this fountain.

17.   How did you get home?

18.   When did John start running so fast?

19.   The chore was done rather slowly.

20.   We will not have an answer immediately.

Directions: Underline the subject once and the verb/verb phrase twice. Cross out
                any prepositional phrases. (Look for **too**, **very**, **so**, **quite**, and **rather**
                within a prepositional phrase.) Circle any adverbs.

1.   She looked inside and outside for her umbrella.

2.   After the dance, everyone went home.

3.   Now and then my very elderly uncle stays with us.

4.   When will you come over to my house?

5.   We jump up and down in exercise class.

6.   Seldom do the children go in and out through that door.

7.   Unfortunately this machine is temporarily out of order.

8.   The lump on his arm is extremely large.

9.   Often we eat lunch here on Saturdays.

10.   Invitations were sent out too early in the week.

11.   The broom couldn't be found anywhere in the garage.

12.   There are five lovely blooms on the flowering plant.

13.   Jill polished her new car very gently.

14.   Where did the experts put the rather ugly trophy?

15.   You did so well in the softball game yesterday.

202

ADVERBS

DEGREES OF ADVERBS

Adverbs often make comparisons.

A.   The **comparative** form compares two *things*.

B.   The **superlative** form compares three or more *things*.

Examples: Bill runs **faster** than I. (**COMPARATIVE** FORM: Bill and I are being compared - 2 people.)

Of the four, Bill runs **fastest**. (**SUPERLATIVE** FORM: four people are being compared.)

There are three ways to form the comparative and the superlative:

A.   **Comparative:**

1.   Add **er** to most one-syllable adverbs.

   fast/faster   hard/harder

2.   Place **more** before most two or more syllable adverbs.*

   slowly/more slowly   favorably/more favorably

3.   Some adverbs totally change form.

   well/better   badly/worse

B.   **Superlative**:

1.   Add **est** to most one-syllable adverbs.

   fast/fastest   hard/hardest

2.   Place **most** before many two or more syllable adverbs.*

   slowly/most slowly   favorably/most favorably

3.   Some adverbs totally change form.

   well/best   badly/worst

*__Less__ for the comparative and **least** for the superlative may also be used.

Adverb	Comparative	Superlative
well	better	best
badly	worse	worst
early	earlier	earliest
rapidly	more rapidly	most rapidly

Directions: Write the required comparative or superlative form in the space provided.

          Example: comparative form of beautifully

          _____more beautifully_____

1.   comparative form of hesitantly

      _____

2.   superlative form of easily

      _____

3.   comparative form of suddenly

      _____

4.   comparative form of soon

      _____

5.   superlative form of badly

      _____

6.   comparative form of weirdly

      _____

7.   superlative form of late

      _____

8.   superlative form of smoothly

      _____

9.   comparative form of carefully

      _____

10.   superlative form of well

      _____

Directions: Select the correct adverb form in the following sentences.

        Example: My parents awake (**earlier**, earliest) than I do.

1.   Of the triplets, Angela waits (more patiently, most patiently).

2.   Glenn laughs (more loudly, most loudly) than his sister.

3.   Melissa hiked (farther, farthest) than Evelyn did.

4.   When our group spotted a snake, Fred reacted (more fearfully, most fearfully).

5.   The manicurist worked (harder, hardest) than the hair stylist.

6.   Of tho twins, he draws (more artistically, most artistically).

7.   I feel (well, better) today than yesterday.

8.   The third appraiser eyed the ring (more closely, most closely).

9.   In our entire class, a left-handed student writes (more legibly, most legibly).

10.   This plant grows (more quickly, most quickly) than that one.

11.   I like this painting (better, best) of the entire display.

12.   That maid cleans (more thoroughly, most thoroughly) than her friend.

13.   This light shines (more brightly, most brightly) of all the lights in our home.

14.   Wilma plays tennis (badder, worse) than Joy.

15.   He deals with us (honester, more honestly).

Directions: Underline the subject once and the verb/verb phrase twice. Cross out any prepositional phrases. (Be sure to look for the adverbs, **quite, too, so,** and **very**, within a prepositional phrase.) Circle any adverbs.

1.   First you must send money to us.

2.   After breakfast we went outside and played in the snow.

3.   Our puppy ran around after its tail.

4.   The cartoonist has been very busy lately.

5.   The pottery in the back will be fired soon.

6.   The business has not done well recently.

7.   That apartment building will be partially completed tomorrow.

8.   A group walked in and sat down quietly.

9.   I have already decided to leave.

10.   Some people become rather angry quite easily.

11.   Turn left at the first traffic signal.

12.   The lady in the very high heels has visited us often.

13.   Now and then I would like an extremely sweet dessert.

14.   Tonight we will go together to the carnival.

15.   She looked upward through the telescope and smiled slightly.

DOUBLE NEGATIVES

<u>**No**</u>, <u>**not**</u>, <u>**never**</u>, <u>**none**</u>, <u>**no one**</u>, <u>**nobody**</u>, <u>**nothing**</u>, <u>**scarcely**</u>, **and** <u>**hardly**</u>
are considered *negative words.** Do not use two of these in an independent
clause.***

Example: Wrong: I do **not** want **nothing**.

Right: I do **not** want anything.
                        OR
            I want **nothing**.

Wrong: I could**n't hardly** hear.

Right: I could**n't** hear.
                        OR
            I could **hardly** hear.

Wrong: He **never** wants **none**.

Right: He **never** wants any.
                        OR
            He wants **none**.

DO NOT "GO" BY SOUND. IF YOU ARE ACCUSTOMED TO
HEARING OR USING DOUBLE NEGATIVES, THEY WILL SOUND
CORRECT.

*<u>Neither</u> is also a negative word and should not be used in the same independent
clause as the others in this list. However, it is fine to use it with the negative
conjunction <u>nor</u> in an independent clause.

Wrong: **Neither** of them like **nobody**.
Right: **Neither** of them like anybody.
Exception: **Neither** plums **nor** apricots were in season.

**An independent clause contains a subject and verb <u>and</u> can stand alone as a
complete thought (sentence).

Directions: Choose the correct answer.

        Example: Those guys don't give (**anyone**, no one) money.

1.   I hadn't (never, ever) seen an alligator before today.

2.   The dolphin did not do (no, any) tricks in the show.

3.   Victor never tells (anything, nothing) that is told to him.

4.   Our school scarcely has (no, any) water fountains.

5.   I don't know (nothing, anything).

6.   The divers (couldn't, could) hardly breathe.

7.   He doesn't want (none, any).

8.   There (is, isn't) scarcely any food in the pantry.

9.   Don't do that (ever, never) again.

10.   They don't want (anybody, nobody) to help them.

11.   Those horses haven't (no, any) water.

12.   I never do (nothing, anything) right.

13.   Neither of the copiers do (anything, nothing) clearly.

14.   Brett doesn't want (nobody, anybody) to tell him what to do.

15.   I don't want (none, any)!

Directions: Choose the correct answer.

Example: I haven't (never, **ever**) toured a prison.

1.   Our cookies (weren't, were) hardly edible.

2.   There wasn't (anyone, no one) in the store.

3.   I don't want (nothing, anything).

4.   Our mail person (hasn't, has) no helpers.

5.   I couldn't take (any, none) with me.

6.   There (weren't, were) scarcely any cookies in the jar.

7.   They will not do it for (nothing, anything).

8.   The patient can't have (any, no) visitors.

9.   Neither of the voters spoke to (nobody, anybody).

10.   I (can't, can) hardly see the board from here.

11.   Some children haven't (never, ever) been to the zoo.

12.   You may not go to (neither, either) place.

13.   I'm doing (nothing, anything) for a whole week.

14.   The photographer shouldn't have waited for (none, any) of the others in
       the group.

15.   I couldn't find (anything, nothing) to read.

A. **Adverb or Adjective?:**

   Directions: Circle the adverb form.

1. crazy, crazily

2. capably, capable

3. courageous, courageously

4. good, well

5. absolutely, absolute

6. careful, carefully

7. safe, safely

B. **Adverbs - How:**

   Directions: Cross out any prepositional phrases.   Underline the subject once
                and verb/verb phrase twice. Label any adverb(s) telling HOW - <u>ADV</u>.
                In the space provided, explain the use of any adverb in the sentence.

1. For a beginning speaker, Horace speaks well.

   _____

2. She stopped abruptly at the entrance to the gated community.

   _____

3. The audience jumped wildly and cheered loudly.

   _____

4. The child chuckled gleefully at her reflection in the mirror.

   _____

Date_____

C. **Adverbs - How:**

Directions: Cross out any prepositional phrases. Underline the subject once and the verb/verb phrase twice. Circle any adverb(s) telling HOW.

1. The criticism was accepted graciously.

2. Can you hit a ball hard?

3. After the symphony, everyone left cheerfully.

D. **Adverbs - When:**

Directions: Cross out any prepositional phrases. Underline the subject once and the verb/verb phrase twice. Label any adverb(s) telling WHEN - ADV. In the space provided, explain the use of any adverb in the sentence.

1. Since her fortieth birthday, Mother never has wanted a party.

_____

2. The travel agent will arrange bus service tomorrow.

_____

3. First, plans for a spring clean-up must be discussed.

_____

E.   **Adverbs - When:**

Directions: Cross out any prepositional phrases. Underline the subject once and the verb/verb phrase twice. Circle any adverb(s) telling WHEN.

1. This toothpaste in a huge tube lasts forever.

2. Sooner or later, someone will give us some help.

3. These awards are presented annually.

F. **Adverbs - Where:**

Directions: Cross out any prepositional phrases. Underline the subject once
and the verb/verb phrase twice. Label any adverb(s) telling
WHERE - ADV. In the space provided, explain the use of any
adverb(s) in the sentence.

1.   That car is rolling backwards!

_____

2.   At the department store, he rode upstairs in an escalator.

_____

3.   The couple fished downstream before lunch.

_____

G. **Adverbs - Where:**

Directions: Cross out any prepositional phrases. Underline the subject once
and the verb/verb phrase twice. Circle any adverb(s) telling
WHERE.

1.   Would you like to go somewhere in an hour?

2.   Please step forward and stop by the sign.

3.   Sherri walked over there near the hot dog stand.

4.   The stewardess drove home from the airport.

H. **Adverbs - to What Extent:**

Directions: Write the seven adverbs that repeatedly tell *to what extent*.

_____

I. **Good or Well?**

Directions: Write **good** or **well** in the space provided.

1. Her grandmother paints ceramics _____.

2. You estimated that answer quite _____.

3. Dr. Barton is a _____ internist.

4. That city in the Midwest has an extremely _____ water system.

5. The colonists governed themselves _____.

6. During the summer months, Charlie was hired by a _____ company.

7. Patricia and Mickey play golf _____ at the Troon course.

8. A _____ turkey dinner often makes us tired.

J. **Adverbs - Double Negatives:**

Directions: Circle the correct answer.

1. Janelle doesn't have (no, any) brothers.

2. His hair hardly ever has (any, no) curl.

3. I don't want (nobody, anybody) to come with me.

4. He hardly ever says (nothing, anything).

5. Herm can't order (anything, nothing).

6. Our friend doesn't (never, ever) go scuba diving.

7. I can't do (anything, nothing) with this!

8. My uncle can't go (nowhere, anywhere) without his camera.

K. **Adverbs:**

Directions: Circle any adverbs.

Suggestion: Cross out any prepositional phrases.   However, check to see if one of the 7 adverbs that tell <u>to what extent</u> may be in any prepositional phrase. If it is, circle it. Underline the subject once and verb/verb phrase twice. Next, go through the sentence looking specifically for any adverbs that tell **how**. Reread the sentence, searching for any adverbs that tell **when**.   Next, look for any adverbs that tell **where**. Finally, look for any adverbs that tell **to what extent** and are not located in a prepositional phrase. Circle any adverb(s).This process may sound long, but once you do it step-by-step, it will become faster and will definitely help you to determine adverbs.

1.   Now, hang on tightly to your seat.

2.   That baby crawls extremely fast across the bare floor.

3.   We shall probably arrive late in the evening.

4.   Gail, upset by the very loud noises, put her work aside.

5.   Today, an eagle flew briskly away from its nest.

6.   Sooner or later, he must grow rather tired from those exercises.

7.   Daily, those roosters crow so loudly.

L.   **Adverbs - Degrees:**

Directions: Circle the correct adverb form.

1.   The winners shot (more often, oftener) than the losing team.

2.   Marcus swam (better, gooder) today than yesterday.

3.   This hula hoop spins (more swiftly, most swiftly) than the yellow one.

4.   Of the entire team, she runs (more slowly, most slowly).

5.   Carry these eggs (more carefully, most carefully) than jelly beans.

6.   Kay acts (more courageous, more courageously) when she's frightened.

214

A. Directions: Cross out any prepositional phrases.   Underline the subject once
               and verb/verb phrase twice.

1. Without Lana's help, we may have to postpone our bake sale.

2. Place this wallpaper up against those cupboards on the back wall.

3. The painter and several workers are not leaving until noon.

B. Directions: Circle the correct adjective form.

1. This speaker seems (more nervous, nervouser) than the preceding one.

2. Your left ankle is (more swollen, most swollen).

3. Of those four kittens, the tiniest is (more playful, most playful).

C. Directions: Write the contraction:

1. cannot - _____   3. it is - _____   5. I am - _____

2. you are - _____   4. I have - _____   6. they will - _____

D. Directions: Cross out any prepositional phrases.   Underline the subject once
               and the verb/verb phrase twice. Write the tense in the blank provided.

1. _____   I shall finish within two hours.

2. _____   Have you been to Vermont?

3. _____   Before the party, Allen made lemon chicken.

4. _____   Throughout the night, those two dogs bark.

5. _____   Heyward will be going to camp during July.

E. Directions: Write A if the noun is abstract; write C if the noun is concrete.

1. ___ bravery   2. ___ garage   3. ___ sympathy   4. ___ steak   5. ___ smog

F. Directions: Write the possessive form:

1. a basketball belonging to four girls: _____

2. a road through the park: _____

3. a gift for a class: _____

4. a decision made by more than one woman: _____

G. Directions: Write <u>N</u> if the boldfaced word is a noun.   Write <u>A</u> if the boldfaced word
serves as an adjective. Write <u>V</u> if the boldfaced word serves as a verb.

1. _____ Several runners darted around a **track** at the local high school.
2. _____ Holly set a **track** record yesterday.
3. _____ We must **track** a course for the car derby.
4. _____ Mia and Joel **star** in many shows.
5. _____ A **star** is fascinating!

H. Directions: Write the past participle form:

1. to shake - _____   5. to sit - _____

2. to leave - _____   6. to rise - _____

3. to give - _____   7. to sink - _____

4. to eat - _____   8. to freeze - _____

I. Directions: Write the plural of each noun:

1. rash - _____   3. bass - _____   5. goose - _____

2. ax - _____   4. fee - _____   6. cross - _____

J. Directions: Label any conjunction or interjection.

1. Great! I've won a new radio or some money.

2. Good heavens! I've locked both my keys and purse in the car!

216

K.   Directions: Cross out any prepositional phrases. Underline the subject once
                   and the verb/verb phrase twice.

1.   The child has (began, begun) to swim.

2.   Have you ever (drank, drunk) pink lemonade?

3.   By Friday, the student will have (ridden, rode) fifty miles back and forth to college.

4.   Mrs. Carlson has (gone, went) to a yard sale.

5.   Each of the pamphlets (has, have) been passed out.

6.   (Rise, Raise) the window shade about four inches.

7.   The member must have (brung, brought) a friend with her.

8.   (May, Can) I look underneath the seat for the lost credit card?

9.   Their newspaper is still (laying, lying) in front of their door.

10. None of the men (has, have) a book concerning French money.

11. Had you (flew, flown) to Atlanta before lunch?

12. She must have (came, come) in very quietly.

13. I might have (broke, broken) this lock accidentally.

14. He could have (lain, laid) the saw under the counter in the workroom.

15. You should have (taken, took) some money along with you.

16. Please, (sit, set) beneath the ramada.

L.   Directions: Cross out any prepositional phrases. Underline the subject once
                   and the verb/verb phrase twice. Write A in the blank if the verb is
                   action, write L if the verb is linking.
Suggestion: Write *is, am, are, was,* or *were* above each verb to help.

1. _____   They feel sad about their neighbor's sick dog.

2. _____   Dave felt the lump on his head.

3. _____   From June to August, the Garr family stays in a cabin by a lake.

4. _____   Her finger stayed red for several days.

M. Directions: List the 23 auxiliary (helping) verbs: _____

_____

_____

N. Directions: Cross out any prepositional phrases. Underline the subject once
and the verb/verb phrase twice. Write the helping verb(s) in column
one and the main verb in column 2.

HELPING VERB(S)   **MAIN VERB**

1. I should not have given that away. _____ _____

2. Everyone of the boys is going. _____ _____

3. He must have left his shoes here. _____ _____

4. Did Brad ask for a new pack? _____ _____

5. Could you move over to the door? _____ _____

O. Directions: Write the 20 linking verbs (12 linking verbs + 8): _____

_____

_____

P. Directions: List the limiting (determining) adjectives.

1. The three articles are _____, _____, and _____.

2. The four demonstratives are _____, _____, _____, and _____.

3. Name the possessive pronouns that can serve as limiting adjectives: _____,

_____, _____, _____, _____, _____, and _____.

4. Give an example of a possessive noun used as a determiner: _____

5. Give an example of a number used as a determiner: _____

6. Five examples of indefinites used as determiners are _____,

_____, _____, _____, and _____.

218

Q. Directions: If the boldfaced word serves as an adjective, write <u>Adj</u>. in the blank.
     If the boldfaced word does not serve as an adjective, write *No*.

1. _____ **Several** new pots and pans were purchased.

2. _____ **Several** will be given awards at the luncheon.

3. _____ **Carl's** is the best!

4. _____ Have you seen **Carl's** salt map?

5. _____ She doesn't like **her** stewed tomatoes.

6. _____ Please give **those** to Maria and Jackson.

R. Directions: Circle any adjectives.

Suggestion: Read each sentence and circle limiting adjectives. Then, circle any descriptive adjectives.

1. A very old brass bed had been sold at that antique auction recently.

2. Many lively children are patiently waiting for their talkative parents.

3. His aunt's bathroom has striped wallpaper with an unusual, orange floral border.

4. Those are two good examples of the disastrous effects of wind erosion.

S. Directions: Box any nouns.

Suggestion: First, locate limiting and descriptive adjectives. Use these to help locate nouns. Then, reread the sentence looking for nouns that appear without an adjective.

1. Jake studies many insects and reptiles in his spare time.

2. This broom and that old rake will be thrown in the garbage on Monday.

3. A friendly dog scampered across the enormous room and licked my hand.

4. Several problems were discussed by the concerned parents during a meeting.

T. Fill in the blank:

1. **The winner is Frank.** Frank is a predicate nominative.   Write a proof:

    Proof: _____

2. **Dad made Mom a wooden shelf.** <u>Mom</u> serves as the _____
    _____ of this sentence.

3. **Fred crushed the can with his foot.** The direct object of this sentence is _____.

4. **A kite had become tangled among some branches.** <u>Branches</u> serves as the
    _____ of the preposition in this sentence.

5. Name a set of correlative conjunctions. _____

U. Directions: Write the sentence type in the space provided.

1. _____ That's right!

2. _____ Is an olive a type of fruit?

3. _____ A tomato is technically a fruit.

4. _____ Finish this assignment.

V. Directions: Write <u>P</u> if the group of words is a phrase; write <u>C</u> if the group of words
                  is a clause.

1. _____ Under the bed.
2. _____ Their house is on Dunbar Lane.
3. _____ When she sings alone.
4. _____ Taking the wrong road.

W. Directions: Write <u>S</u> if the group of words is a sentence. Write <u>F</u> if the group of
                  words is a fragment. Write <u>R-O</u> if the group of words is a run-on.

1. _____ Harold after the last speech.
2. _____ They have a cat, it's a Siamese.
3. _____ Has this floor been washed?

220

PRONOUNS

Pronouns take the place of nouns. They agree in number and gender.

PERSONAL PRONOUNS:

Nominative Pronouns (Subjective Pronouns)	**Objective Pronouns**	**Possessive Pronouns**
I	me	my, mine
he	him	his
she	her	her, hers
you	you	your, yours
it	it	it, its
we	us	our, ours
they	them	their, theirs
who	whom	whose

FUNCTION IN A SENTENCE:

1. SUBJECT

2. PREDICATE NOMINATIVE

FUNCTION IN A SENTENCE:

1. OBJECT OF THE PREPOSITION

2. DIRECT OBJECT

3. INDIRECT OBJECT

FUNCTION IN A SENTENCE:

SHOW OWNERSHIP

PRONOUNS

Personal Pronouns / Nominative Pronouns:

The nominative pronouns are **I**, **he**, **she**, **you**, **it**, **we**, **they**, and **who**.

Look at your pronoun chart. There are only two pronouns that are in both the nominative and objective columns: **you** and **it**. These are called neutral pronouns and do not change from nominative to objective form.

NOMINATIVE PRONOUNS FUNCTION AS EITHER THE SUBJECT OR PREDICATE NOMINATIVE IN A SENTENCE.

A.   Review of Subjects:

The subject of a sentence, in easiest terms, is <u>who</u> or <u>what</u> the sentence is about.

      Examples: That <u>handle</u> is broken.

                     <u>We</u> have not begun a new project.

B.   Review of Predicate Nominatives:

The predicate nominative is the same as the subject of the sentence.   To check a predicate nominative, try inverting the sentence.

                                  PN
      Examples: That <u>lady</u> is my sister.

          <u>My sister is that lady.</u>

                             PN
      The <u>winner</u> was she.

          <u>She was the winner.</u>

Note: Be sure to use the inverted form with pronouns. Perhaps you have heard someone say something like, "The winner was her." <u>Her</u> has to be wrong because the inverted form would read, "Her is the winner."

Directions: Cross out any prepositional phrases. Underline the subject once and the verb/verb phrase twice.

Example: <u>Bill</u> and <u>I</u> <u>have gone</u> ~~with Uncle Fred~~.

1.   May Clarene and I go to the store?

2.   We must have lost his phone number.

3.   The hikers and we might try to climb that mountain.

4.   Did she place the garden hose by the fountain?

5.   Jeremy, Joshua, Julie, and I should have prepared the meal.

6.   In the middle of the night, they left for Baton Rouge, Louisiana.

7.   Nancy and I cannot carry this package.

8.   Have you ever taken gymnastics?

9.   After the show, we went out for pizza.

10.   Did they ask for more information.

11.   Those leaders and we are in charge of the social hour.

12.   Either Mother or I will be attending the meeting.

13.   It is a rather hot, muggy day.

14.   You could have shined all of the silver for me.

15.   My father and I haven't ever camped beside a river.

Directions: Cross out any prepositional phrases. Underline the subject once and the verb/verb phrase twice. Label any predicate nominative(s) - PN. Then write the inverted form of the sentence on the line provided.

PN
Example: The <u>lady</u> ~~in the red dress~~ <u>is</u> Flora's agent.
  Check: <u>Flora's agent is the lady in the red dress.</u>

1.   Justin Harper is my friend.
     _____

2.   Justin Harper is he.
     _____

3.   The loser is Wanda.
     _____

4.   The loser is she.
     _____

5.   My lawyer is the man in the brown suit.
     _____

6.   My lawyer is he in the brown suit.
     _____

7.   The runners in that race are the Hinkle twins.
     _____

8.   The runners in that race are they.
     _____

9.   The next person in line should be _____(your name).
     _____

10. The next person in line should be I.
     _____

Name_____   **PRONOUNS**
                                          Subject or Predicate
Date_____   Nominative?

Directions: Write <u>S</u> on the line if the underlined pronoun is the subject of the
             sentence. Write <u>PN</u> on the line provided if the underlined pronoun is the
             predicate nominative of the sentence.

             Example: __S__   1.   Do <u>you</u> want a bike?

_____   1.   The security guard and <u>I</u> searched the building.

_____   2.   <u>They</u> will not be fishing in that lake.

_____   3.   Our student council officers are those three and <u>I</u>.

_____   4.   <u>He</u> was not in class this morning.

_____   5.   The last ones to finish were <u>we</u>.

_____   6.   Have <u>you</u> lived in Miami long?

_____   7.   <u>We</u> could not go to the computer center today.

_____   8.   The next debaters will be Fred and <u>I</u>.

_____   9.   The guest speaker was <u>she</u> in the second row.

_____   10.   <u>It</u> might have worked out for all of us.

_____   11.   The members of the swimming team are <u>they</u> in the red.

_____   12.   Yesterday, the last person selected was <u>I</u>.

_____   13.   Maybe <u>we</u> could ride the rollercoaster next.

_____   14.   The ones recommended for the job are <u>he</u> and <u>she</u>.

_____   15.   Could <u>it</u> be possible?

PRONOUNS

Personal Pronouns / Objective Case:

The objective pronouns are **me**, **him**, **her**, **you**, **it**, **us**, **them** and **whom**.

Look at your pronoun chart. There are only two pronouns that are in both the objective and nominative columns: **you** and **it**. These are called neutral pronouns and do not change forms.

OBJECTIVE PRONOUNS FUNCTION AS ONE OF THE FOLLOWING:

  A. Object of the Preposition
  B. Direct Object
  C. Indirect Object

A. Review of Object of the Preposition:

The object of the preposition is the noun or pronoun that follows a preposition.

Examples: Stay *in your* **room**.

Go *with* **me**.

B. Review of Direct Object:

A direct object receives the action of the verb.

                    D.O.
Examples: I dropped the **eggs**.

                    D.O.
The dog licked **me**.

C. Review of Indirect Object:

The indirect object "indirectly" receives a direct object. "To" or "for" can be inserted mentally before an indirect object.

Examples: The baker made Mother a pie.
                 for **I.O.**
The baker made / **Mother** a pie.

Our grocer gave her coupons.
                 to **I.O.**
Our grocer gave / **her** coupons.

Directions: Cross out any prepositional phrases. Label any object of the
preposition - <u>O.P.</u> Underline the subject once and the verb/verb phrase
twice in each sentence.

                              O.P.
    Example: Everyone ~~except me~~ left immediately.

1.   Please do that for me.

2.   The wind blew against him during the storm.

3.   Does the new teacher live near you?

4.   Joshua ate lunch beside me today.

5.   The bus left without her.

6.   A bullet whizzed past them.

7.   The story was all about us.

8.   Have you received a letter from me?

9.   The crew docked the boat and went inside it.

10.   The gift was sent to them yesterday.

11.   He often chases after us.

12.   Their relatives go with them on vacations.

13.   Bob sits behind Ross and me.

14.   A bicycle was lying along the side of the road.

15.   Do you want me to go with you?*

*To + verb = infinitive

To go is an infinitive (not a prepositional phrase).

Directions: Cross out any prepositional phrases. Underline the subject once and the verb/verb phrase twice. Label any direct object - D.O.

Example: We picked flowers in the meadow.

1.   A chicken scratched the ground for food.

2.   They baked the chicken in the oven.

3.   The pen pal wrote a long letter.

4.   Jeremy erased the marks from his paper.

5.   Mother put all the tea bags in a canister.

6.   The child hit the ball hard.

7.   The judge selected it as the best.

8.   A bee stung me.

9.   The mayor telephoned us with his concerns.

10.   Some art enthusiasts purchased them for their homes.

11.   Has the movie frightened you?

12.   A fun-loving youngster threw her into the pool.

13.   That person followed William and me home.

14.   I sent it to the wrong address.

15.   Their parents sent the triplets and her to Cypress Gardens.

Directions: Underline the subject once and the verb/verb phrase twice. Label a
direct object - D.O.   Label an indirect object - I.O.

I.O.   D.O.
Example: Kirk sent the senator a letter.

1.   Mack gave the teacher a note from his father.

2.   Grace tossed me a cookie.

3.   The company sent them the wrong order.

4.   Mrs. Brewster gave us some peanut candy.

5.   The nurse brought me a television to watch.

6.   Send him the best recorder in your store.

7.   The bank offered Chuck and me a loan for our business.

8.   He left us a fifty dollar bill on the entryway table.

9.   A tall waiter served us our dinner.

10.   The teacher gave the class a test.

11.   During the night, someone passed us two blankets.

12.   The person on the end passed Rachel and us some popcorn.

Directions: Select the correct pronoun.

Example: (**They**, Them) surely are great slides.

1.   Someone must sit near (I, me).

2.   (We, Us) want a new kite.

3.   The kitten followed (we, us).

4.   Our principal presented Tom and (I, me) awards.

5.   My father and (I, me) refinished an old cart.

6.   The applicants for that job were Frank and (I, me).

7.   Who bought (they, them) a magazine?

8.   Rosa asked (they, them) a question.

9.   My partner and (I, me) agreed to meet at six o'clock.

10.   Our best actors are Cliff and (she, her).

11.   Someone gave (we, us) a new picture.

12.   The cat scratches (she, her) nearly every day.

13.   Did anyone discuss the subject with (he, him)?

14.   Great Grandpa sent (they, them) airplane tickets to Seattle.

15.   Will you take (I, me) to Hong Kong?

Name_____

Date_____

Directions: Write the function of the underlined pronoun in the space provided. Use
the following abbreviations:
D.O. = Direct Object
I. O. = Indirect Object
P. N. = Predicate Nominative
O. P. = Object of the Preposition
S. = Subject

Example: ___I.O.___ The child made <u>me</u> a mud pie.

Remember: The pronouns **I, he, she, we, they,** and **who** function as either a
subject or a predicate nominative.

The pronouns **me, him, her, us, them,** and **whom** function as either a
direct object, an indirect object, or an object of the preposition.

The pronouns **you** and **it** can function as a subject, a predicate
nominative, a direct object, an indirect object, or an object of the
preposition.

_____ 1. Someone must sit near <u>me</u>.

_____ 2. <u>We</u> want a new kite.

_____ 3. The kitten followed <u>us</u>.

_____ 4. Our principal presented Tom and <u>me</u> awards.

_____ 5. The applicants for the job were Frank and <u>I</u>.

_____ 6. Who bought <u>them</u> a magazine?

_____ 7. Our best actors are Cliff and <u>she</u>.

_____ 8. The cat scratches <u>her</u> nearly every day.

_____ 9. Did anyone discuss the subject with <u>him</u>?

_____ 10. Will you take <u>me</u> to Hong Kong?

PRONOUNS

Personal Pronouns / Possessives:

The possessive pronouns are: **my, mine**

                                         his

                                       her, hers

                                       your, yours

                                       its

                                       our, ours

                                     their, theirs

                                     whose

A. **My**, **his**, **her**, **your**, **its**, **our**, **their**, and **whose** are used before nouns and other pronouns and are often called possessive adjectives.

    Examples: Has **my** *book* been found?

                         His *house* is painted yearly.

                         Your *watch* is incorrect.

                         A lion licked **its** *paws*.

                         Has **our** *mail* been delivered?

                         Their *cars* weren't in the driveway.

B. **Mine**, **hers**, **yours**, **ours**, **and** **theirs** do not usually come before a noun or pronoun but refer back to it in the sentence.

    Examples: Those *journals* are **mine**.

                         Is this *cup* **yours**?

                         A cream-colored *car* is **hers**.

                         That tree *house* is **ours**.

C. **The possessivie his occurs in the same form before and after a noun or pronoun.**

    Example: **His** *plan* succeeded.

                         Those *models* are **his**.

PRONOUNS

Personal Pronouns / Possessives:

Possessive Pronouns do **NOT** have an apostrophe (**'**).

A.   **It's** is not a possessive pronoun: **it's = it + is**

   Its is a possessive pronoun. Example: The bird drank **its** water.

   Suggestion: If you are unsure if <u>its</u> or <u>it's</u> should be used, read the
   sentence with the <u>it's</u> (it is) form. Trust SOUND to determine
   the correct form.

Example:	<u>It's</u> hot.
Check:	It is hot.

Example:	The bird drank <u>it's</u> water.
Check:	The bird drank it is water.
Correct:	The bird drank <u>its</u> water.

B.   **You're** is not a possessive pronoun: **you're = you + are**

   Your is a possessive pronoun.   Example: What is **your** name?

   Suggestion: If you are unsure if <u>you're</u> or <u>your</u> should be used, read the
   sentence with the <u>you're</u> form. Trust SOUND to determine
   the correct form.

Example:	<u>You're</u> the greatest.
Check:	You are the greatest.

Example:	<u>You're</u> shoe is untied.
Check:	You are shoe is untied.
Correct:	<u>Your</u> shoe is untied.

PRONOUNS

Personal Pronouns / Possessives:

Possessive Pronouns do **NOT** have an apostrophe (').

C.   **They're** is not a possessive pronoun: **They're = They + are**

Their is a possessive pronoun. Example: **Their** house is old.

Suggestion: If you are unsure if <u>they're</u> or <u>their</u> should be used,
read the sentence with the <u>they're</u> (they are) form.
Trust SOUND to determine the correct form.

Example:	<u>They're</u> playing checkers.
Check:	They are playing checkers.

Example:	<u>They're</u> house is old.
Check:	They are house is old.
Correct:	<u>Their</u> house is old.

Name_____ **PRONOUNS**

Date_____

Directions: Select the correct pronoun.

Example: (**It's**, Its) a rainy day.

1.   (You're, Your) copies are ready.

2.   Marcy wanted to know if (they're, their) coming.

3.   A giraffe ate (it's, its) dinner.

4.   Did they ask if (you're, your) going?

5.   (They're, Their) house is the fourth one on Arbor Lane.

6.   Do you think that (it's, its) possible?

7.   (Who's, Whose) the new student?

8.   I think that (they're, their) plans have changed.

9.   (Who's, Whose) foot did I just step on?

10.   Has the peacock lost some of (it's, its) feathers?

11.   (You're, Your) not supposed to throw that.

12.   Has anyone told them that (they're, their) allowed to go?

13.   Our group hasn't decided (who's, whose) advice to follow.

14.   Does Molly like (you're, your) choice of colors?

15.   Give me that if (it's, its) dry.

PRONOUNS

Antecedents:

An antecedent is the noun or pronoun to which a possessive or a reflexive pronoun refers back in the sentence.

Example: That dog lost <u>its</u> collar.

    A.   The pronoun <u>its</u> refers back to **dog**.
           (The dog lost the dog's collar.)

    B.   **Dog** is the noun <u>its</u> refers back to in the sentence.

    C.   **Dog** is the antecedent.

Example: Some ducklings waddled after <u>their</u> mother.

    A.   The pronoun <u>their</u> refers back to **ducklings**.
           (Some ducklings waddled after the ducklings' mother.)

    B.   **Ducklings** is the noun <u>their</u> refers back to in the sentence.

    C.   **Ducklings** is the antecedent.

Example: Has anyone lost <u>his</u> comb?

    A.   The pronoun <u>his</u> refers back to **anyone**.
           (Has anyone lost anyone's comb?)

    B.   **Anyone** is the pronoun <u>his</u> refers back to in the sentence.

    C.   **Anyone** is the antecedent.

PRONOUNS
Antecedents

Directions: In the space provided, write the antecedent for the boldfaced word.

Example: ___monkey___   1.   A monkey hurt **its** arm.

1. _____   The little girl broke **her** foot on the slide.

2. _____   The furniture movers left **their** truck in the driveway.

3. _____   Will and I don't want **our** meals.

4. _____   Has the trucker finished **his** trip?

5. _____   A few students left **their** notebooks in the library.

6. _____   A large, black spider spun **its** web.

7. _____   He finished **his** photo album today.

8. _____   The women left **their** office.

9. _____   They handed in **their** final exams.

10. _____   A lamb lost **its** way back to the barn.

Directions: In the space provided, write the antecedent for the boldfaced word.

Example: ___student___   A student cleaned out **her** desk.

_____   1.   Our club held **its** annual car wash.

_____   2.   Has Dad worn **his** new suit yet?

_____   3.   I don't want **my** dinner.

_____   4.   The clerks were on **their** break.

_____   5.   Stacy left **her** surfboard here.

_____   6.   Nobody has **his** radio tuned into that station.

_____   7.   You must send **your** cards early.

_____   8.   Some squirrels were playing in **their** tree.

_____   9.   Susan and Zak enjoy **their** karate lessons.

_____   10.   A bird fluttered **its** wings and flew off.

_____   11.   My brother and I want **our** own phone.

_____   12.   Antonio cooked **his** own breakfast.

_____   13.   A plant manufactures **its** own food.

_____   14.   Someone has forgotten to do **her** chore.

_____   15.   Three pilots purchased **their** own plane.

PRONOUNS

Reflexive Pronouns:

Reflexive pronouns are **myself, himself, herself, itself, yourself, ourselves,** and **themselves**.

Hisself and **theirselves** are incorrect. Never use them.

Reflexive pronouns reflect back to another noun or pronoun in the sentence. A reflexive pronoun will have an antecedent.

        Examples: A.   The <u>lady</u> washed the car **herself.**

                         (<u>Lady</u> is the noun antecedent to which the reflexive pronoun, **herself**, refers.)

                  B.   Can <u>you</u> fix the tire **yourself**?

                         (<u>You</u> is the pronoun antecedent to which the reflexive pronoun, **yourself**, refers.)

                  C.   That <u>machine</u> automatically shuts **itself** off.

                         (<u>Machine</u> is the noun antecedent to which the reflexive pronoun, **itself**, refers.)

Directions: Circle any reflexive pronoun(s) in each sentence.

1.   Do you prefer to handle that yourself?

2.   The child remarked, "I will do this myself."

3.   Did the carpenters enjoy building the cabin themselves?

4.   The mower turns itself off automatically.

5.   We, ourselves, must choose the goals.

6.   Let Grant speak to Mr. Jones himself.

7.   I want to tackle this task myself.

8.   Janet and I have only ourselves to blame.

9.   A yellow canary perched itself on the top rung.

10.   Has anyone ever tried this herself?

11.   Richard often talks to himself.

12.   They patted themselves on the back for a job well done.

13.   She would not allow herself to face defeat.

14.   I refuse to do it myself.

15.   Walter's dad built the cabinets himself.

16.   The cat licked itself.

17.   Do you want to do it yourself?

18.   We enjoyed ourselves at the party.

19.   The children made the cookies themselves.

20.   That machine will not repeat itself during a power failure.

PRONOUNS

Demonstrative Pronouns:

Demonstrative pronouns are **this, that, these,** and **those.**

        Examples: I want **that.**

                        This is a pitted spoon.

                        Are **these** supposed to be here?

                        Those became ruined when washed in hot water.

If **this, that, these,** or **those** modify or go over to a noun or another pronoun, they are adjectives.

        Examples: A.   *This* trim is crooked. (**This** is an adjective: this trim.)

                                This is crooked. (**This** is a pronoun.)

                    B.   Did you enjoy *that* play? (**That** is an adjective: that play.)

                                Did you enjoy **that**? (**That** is a pronoun.)

                    C.   Give me *those* ornaments. (**Those** is an adjective: those ornaments.)

                                Give me **those**.   (**Those** is a pronoun.)

                    D.   Bring *these* bars with you.   (**These** is an adjective: these bars.)

                                Bring **these** with you. (**These** is a pronoun.)

Directions: Write <u>P</u> on theline provided if the underlined word serves as a pronoun in the sentence. Write <u>A</u> on the line provided if the underlined word serves as an adjective in the sentence.

Example: __P__   Do you want <u>this</u> on your sandwich?

_____   1.   <u>Those</u> candles burn brightly.

_____   2.   Give me <u>that</u>, please.

_____   3.   Does <u>this</u> fence need to be repaired?

_____   4.   In a few days <u>these</u> avocados will be ripe.

_____   5.   <u>That</u> fly landed on my arm.

_____   6.   Pull <u>those</u> down over your feet.

_____   7.   I think <u>that</u> answer should be forty-four.

_____   8.   Are <u>these</u> the ones you wanted?

_____   9.   I will give you <u>this</u> for your sixteenth birthday.

_____   10.   <u>This</u> one must have been lost for a long time.

_____   11.   My brother gave me <u>those</u> four magnets.

_____   12.   Carrie might be able to use <u>those</u> for the party.

_____   13.   How did you know <u>that</u>, Irving?

_____   14.   <u>These</u> onions are making me cry.

_____   15.   Grandmother says she enjoys doing <u>this</u> for us.

PRONOUNS

Interrogative Pronouns:

Interrogative pronouns are **who**, **whom**, **whose**, **which**, and **what**.

Interrogative pronouns ask a question.

Examples: **Who** is your favorite singer?

To **whom** do I give my tray?

Whose is that?

Which will Samantha select?

What is your opinion?

Who is in the nominative case and will serve as either a subject or a predicate nominative.

Examples: **Who** won?   (subject)

The winner is **who**?   (predicate nominative)

Whom is in the objective case and will serve as a direct object, an indirect object, or an object of the preposition.

Examples: To **whom** did you reply?   (object of the preposition)

The florist sent **whom** that corsage?   (indirect object)

The teacher chose **whom**?   (direct object)

Whose, which, and **what** are pronouns when they stand alone. However, if they modify (go over to) a noun or another pronoun, they function as adjectives.

Examples: **Whose** has been selected?   (pronoun)

Whose *paper* is on the floor?   (adjective: whose paper)

Which do we need?   (pronoun)

Which *one* looks better?   (adjective: which one)

Directions: Write P on the line if the boldfaced word serves as a pronoun. Write A on the line if the boldfaced word serves as an adjective.

  Example: __P__   **Which** do you prefer?

_____ 1. **Whose** coat is this?

_____ 2. **What** is your answer?

_____ 3. **Whose** are these?

_____ 4. **Which** car are you buying?

_____ 5. **What** are you doing?

_____ 6. Do you know **whose** dog this is?

_____ 7. **Which** does Maryanne want?

_____ 8. **What** rock group do you like best?

_____ 9. **Which** one have you decided upon?

_____ 10. You said **what**?

Directions: Select the correct answer.

  Example: (**Who**, Whom) is your friend?

1. To (who, whom) do I give my money?

2. (Who, Whom) will be our next club president?

3. Dad gave the tickets to (who, whom)?

4. The winner was (who, whom)?

PRONOUNS

Indefinite Pronouns:

Indefinite pronouns are **some**, **many**, **few**, **several**, **each**, **both**, **either**, **neither**, **someone**, **somebody**, **anyone**, **anybody**, **nobody**, **everyone**, **everybody**, **any**, and **none**.

Examples: **Some** will be expected to participate.

Are there **many** in the ice chest?

A **few** said no.

Several have already received scholarships.

Each must learn a new step in that dance.

I'll take **both**.

We don't want **either**.

Neither has been eating much today.

Ask **someone** to drive you to school.

Did Mindy tell **somebody** about the incident?

Would **anyone** like to take a helicopter ride?

Anybody may join.

Nobody talks during a movie.

My neighbor seems to know **everyone**.

Everybody was having a good time.

They don't think that he has **any** left.

Although the baked beans smelled good, I wanted **none**.

Pronoun or Adjective:

If **some, many, few, several, each, both, either, neither, someone, somebody, anyone, anybody, nobody, everyone, everybody, and any** modify (go over to) a noun or pronoun, they function as adjectives instead of pronouns.

Examples: **Many** *ribbons* were given.
A **few** *pancakes* remained on the plate.
Everyone's *cars* were parked along the street.
Both *envelopes* were unopened.
Does he want **any** *juice* ?

Name_____

Date_____

Directions: Write <u>P</u> on the line if the boldfaced word serves as a pronoun. Write <u>A</u> on
              the line if the boldfaced word serves as an adjective.

Example: ___A___   **Some** people never learn.

_____ 1.   **Both** dogs are German shepherds.

_____ 2.   Do you like **both**?

_____ 3.   I want one of **each** please.

_____ 4.   I think that **each** speaker was interesting.

_____ 5.   A **few** projects were on display.

_____ 6.   There were only a **few** left.

_____ 7.   **Everyone's** luggage was aboard the plane.

_____ 8.   The announcer told **everyone** about the change in schedule.

_____ 9.   Are there **several** who aren't coming with us?

_____ 10. The visitors toured our city **several** times.

_____ 11. **Many** ants were crawling on the ground.

_____ 12. Had **many** fallen at the skating rink?

_____ 13. Does **anyone** have the time?

_____ 14. Is this **anyone's** pen?

_____ 15. There are **some** hot dogs in the freezer.

_____ 16. **Some** enjoy the harbor cruise at night.

Name_____

Date_____

Directions: Write <u>P</u> on the line if the boldfaced word serves as a pronoun. Write <u>A</u> on the line if the boldfaced word serves as an adjective.

Example: __A__   **Few** animals hang by their tails.

_____ 1.   Will you take **both** with you?

_____ 2.   **Several** have been sold recently.

_____ 3.   **Some** shrimp boats returned to shore.

_____ 4.   This may take **several** hours.

_____ 5.   Is **everyone** ready?

_____ 6.   That is **nobody's** idea of a joke.

_____ 7.   I'll take a **few** of those.

_____ 8.   How **many** do you want?

_____ 9.   I have **none**.

_____ 10. The box didn't have **any** top.

_____ 11. **Each** must take his turn at the swings.

_____ 12. Has **anyone** seen my checkbook?

_____ 13. That game was fun for **both** participants.

_____ 14. **Neither** of them is allowed beyond this point.

_____ 15. **Somebody's** shoe is under the couch.

PRONOUNS

Indefinite Pronouns:

A.   **Some, many, few, several,** and **both** are plural pronouns.

In making subject and verb agree, do not add **s** to the verb.

Examples: <u>Both</u> <u>like</u> the same styles.   (present tense)

<u>Several</u> <u>feel</u> sorry for leaving early.   (present tense)

<u>Some</u> <u>liked</u> the idea.   (past tense)

<u>The possessive pronoun **their** is used with **some, many, few,** and **several**</u>.

B.   **Each, either, neither, someone, somebody, anyone, anybody,**

nobody, everyone, everybody, one, no one, another, anything, and

nothing are singular pronouns.

In making subject and verb agree, add **s** to most verb forms in the present
tense.

Examples: <u>Each</u> <u>likes</u> the new pony.   (present tense)

<u>Nobody</u> <u>writes</u> to me.   (present tense)

<u>Everybody</u> <u>jogged</u> a mile.   (past tense)

<u>The possessive pronouns **her, his,** or **its** are used with singular pronouns</u>.

PRONOUNS

Indefinite Pronouns:

C.   The possessive pronouns **his, her,** and **its** are used with singular indefinite pronouns: **each, either, neither, someone, somebody, anyone, anybody, nobody, no one,** and **another.**

Examples: **Each** chooses <u>his</u> own course of study.

Either of the clowns has <u>his</u> own popcorn stand.

Neither of the teams won <u>its</u> championship.

Someone shared <u>her</u> lunch with me.

Somebody left <u>her</u> wallet on the step.

One left <u>its</u> nest.

Everyone must leave <u>his</u> book on the desk

Has **anyone** decided on <u>her</u> choice of desserts?

Everybody needs <u>his</u> pencil and pen.

No one brought <u>her</u> towel to the pool.

<u>In making subject and verb agree, be sure to find the subject by crossing out prepositional phrases.</u>

Examples: <u>One</u> ~~of the girls~~ <u>speaks</u> ~~with an accent~~.

<u>Either</u> ~~of the books~~ <u>is</u> a good choice.

<u>Each</u> ~~of the triplets~~ <u>wants</u> *her* own room.

Directions: Circle the correct answer.

1.   Few took (his, their) shoes to the beach.

2.   Somebody must give (his, their) bread to the birds.

3.   Each needs to bring (her, their) towel to the pool.

4.   Someone has lost (her, their) purse.

5.   Several should have sent (his, their) letters today.

6.   Did either of the children share (his, their) toys?

7.   Everybody should take (his, their) time.

8.   Has either of the snakes shed (its, their) skin?

9.   Many want to leave (her, their) cars in the parking garage.

10.   Neither wants (her, their) boots on.

11.   Nobody wanted to prepare (his, their) own lunch.

12.   Did everyone remember to bring (his, their) jacket?

13.   One of the girls has given (her, their) saxophone to a friend.

14.   Marcia and Todd have not had (there, their) tetanus shots yet.

15.   Neither of the doctors has (his, their) office downtown.

Directions: Circle the correct answer.

1.   Everyone could not bring (his, their) pet to the program.

2.   Neither wants (her, their) statements published.

3.   In the fall, a few trees shed (its, their) leaves.

4.   In the dark of the night, nobody wants to leave (his, their) nice, warm bed.

5.   Have many given you (her, their) dues?

6.   Be sure that each does (her, their) required number of sit-ups.

7.   Had either of the dogs had (its, their) tail clipped?

8.   Several of the shoppers gave (his, their) opinions about the new product.

9.   May everybody read (his, their) book for fifteen minutes?

10.   Both are taking (her, their) tents in the small canoe.

11.   We have a few who purchased (his, their) own clothes.

12.   Will someone give me (his, their) pencil?

13.   Did one of the books have (its, their) cover missing?

14.   Some will want (his, their) way constantly.

15.   Everybody must take (his, their) books.

Directions: Circle the correct answer.

1.   Each (know, knows) the correct answer.

2.   Nobody (need, needs) to do that tonight.

3.   Several (guide, guides) people through the historic park.

4.   Everyone (bring, brings) his lunch on Fridays.

5.   Few (eat, eats) there.

6.   Either (ride, rides) a bus downtown.

7.   One (crawl, crawls) , and the other baby walks.

8.   Neither of the musicians (play, plays) the guitar.

9.   Some (walk, walks) three miles every day.

10.   During the day, many (choose, chooses) to stay indoors.

11.   Someone (has, have) a new motorcycle.

12.   Someone (read, reads) to the children nightly.

13.   Both (create, creates) a problem.

14.   After the game, no one (go, goes) there anymore.

15.   Either of the fans (work, works).

A. **Subject or Predicate Nominative?**

Directions: Write <u>S</u> if the pronoun in boldfaced print functions as the subject; write <u>PN</u> if the pronoun in boldfaced print functions as a predicate nominative.

Suggestion: **Cross out any prepositional phrase(s). Underline the subject once and the verb/verb phrase twice. Then, make your decision.**

Remember: **Invert the sentence to prove a predicate nominative.**

1. _____   Ralph and **I** will be attending the governor's meeting.

2. _____   The wisest church elder is **he** in the dark blue suit.

3. _____   Our guest for the spring festival will be **she**.

4. _____   Perhaps **you** should add a few more drops of oil to the vinegar.

B. **Objective Pronouns:**

Directions: Choose the letter that tells how the pronoun in boldfaced print functions in the sentence.

1. _____   The soccer ball hit **her** in the head.
       a.   object of the preposition
       b.   direct object
       c.   indirect object

2. _____   Please give **them** a copy of the report.
       a.   object of the preposition
       b.   direct object
       c.   indirect object

3. _____   Sit beside **me**!
       a.   object of the preposition
       b.   direct object
       c.   indirect object

C. **Using Nominative and Objective Pronouns:**
   Directions: Choose the correct word.

1. Tell (I, me) your phone number.

2. Does (she, her) go to the library weekly?

3. His mother looked at (he, him) with a frown.

4. The lady gave (we, us) shoppers some coupons.

5. The forest ranger is (him, he) standing by the truck.

6. The pastor's wife is (she, her) in the flowered dress.

7. A paper airplane landed between Timothy and (I, me).

8. The chef prepared (we, us) a special salad without meat.

9. One of the greatest Cubs fans was (me, I).

D. **Pronouns in Compounds:**
   Directions: Choose the correct word.
Suggestion: You may want to cover the first part of the compound.

1. Rick and (I, me) went to the zoo.

2. The clerk handed Mrs. Jones and (them, they) several bags.

3. Give Stan and (he, him) money for the tickets.

4. My cousins are Yvonne and (she, her).

5. Some children sat near the sunbathers and (we, us).

6. His mother and (we, us) watched an air show.

7. The coach patted Jason and (I, me) on the back.

8. Programs were handed to parents and (they, them).

E. **Possessives:**

Directions: Select the correct word.

1. (Your, You're) so funny.

2. I want to know if (their, they're) sincere about helping.

3. (Its, It's) foot was caught in a trap.

4. (Your, You're) hair needs to be cut.

F. **Antecedents:**

Directions: Write the antecedent of the boldfaced pronoun.

1. _____ Bridgette wants to bring **her** dog along.

2. _____ Must I carry these bags **myself**?

3. _____ We like **our** relatives.

4. _____ The boy wants to do the puzzle **himself**.

5. _____ Mrs. Elles and her friend are taking **their** time.

G. **Pronouns:**

Directions: Fill in the blank.

1. Write two examples of demonstrative pronouns: _____ and _____.

2. Write two examples of interrogative pronouns: _____ and _____.

3. Write two examples of reflexive pronouns: _____ and _____.

4. Write two examples of indefinite pronouns: _____ and _____.

5. Write two examples of possessive pronouns: _____ and _____.

H. **Demonstrative, Interrogative, and Indefinite Pronouns:**

Directions: Write <u>A</u> if the boldfaced word serves as an adjective; write <u>P</u> if
the boldfaced word serves as a pronoun.

1. _____   **Several** will be for sale just before the holidays.
2. _____   Please bring **several** dollars with you to the event.
3. _____   **That** is a very unusual parrot.
4. _____   I didn't know **that** fact about Queen Elizabeth.
5. _____   **Few** chose to hike Pinnacle Peak.
6. _____   **Few** beavers live in that creek.
7. _____   **What** is your middle name?
8. _____   To **which** public library do you go?
9. _____   Would you like **these**?
10. _____   Are **these** cuff links silver?

I. **Pronouns:**

Directions: Circle the correct pronoun.

1. (Who, Whom) is the judge?
2. They want to color the map (themselves, theirselves).
3. Mr. Helman and (us, we) have agreed to a settlement.
4. Did the bridal company and (they, them) meet to discuss marriage details?
5. With (who, whom) are you working?
6. The scout leader gave Kit, Ryan, and (she, her) a badge.
7. One of the girls left (their, her) luggage at the airport.
8. The owner of the new cafe is (she, her) holding the menus.
9. Please give (we, us) details about your happy childhood memories.
10. Everyone of the boys needs (his, their) jacket.
11. The magazine company sent (they, them) a reminder to renew their subscription.
12. The students chose (who, whom) as their leader?

256

Name_____ **CUMULATIVE REVIEW**
Pronoun Unit

Date_____

A. Directions: Write the sentence type.

1. _____ Please wash off the table.

2. _____ How many days are in February?

3. _____ A rock collection is on the top shelf of his desk.

4. _____ You're right!

B. Directions: Write fifty prepositions.

1. _____   14. _____   27. _____   40. _____

2. _____   15. _____   28. _____   41. _____

3. _____   16. _____   29. _____   42. _____

4. _____   17. _____   30. _____   43. _____

5. _____   18. _____   31. _____   44. _____

6. _____   19. _____   32. _____   45. _____

7. _____   20. _____   33. _____   46. _____

8. _____   21. _____   34. _____   47. _____

9. _____   22. _____   35. _____   48. _____

10. _____   23. _____   36. _____   49. _____

11. _____   24. _____   37. _____   50. _____

12. _____   25. _____   38. _____

13. _____   26. _____   39. _____

C. Directions: Write <u>S</u> if the group of words is a sentence, write <u>F</u> if the group of words is a fragment, and write <u>R-O</u> if the group of words is a run-on.

1. _____ His head aches terribly.

2. _____ Farnsworth likes to play two-square, his sister enjoys tag.

3. _____ Jerry during the winter storm.

4. _____ After the students learned about the Aztecs of Mexico.

D. Directions: Write the twenty-three helping verbs.

_____

_____

E. Directions: Write the contraction.

1. will not - _____   4. who is - _____   7. he is - _____

2. cannot - _____   5. they are - _____   8. it is - _____

3. you will - _____   6. I am - _____   9. has not - _____

F. Directions: Write the plural of each noun.

1. leaf - _____   3. repair - _____   5. fly - _____

2. deer - _____   4. tomato - _____   6. proof - _____

G. Directions: Circle any abstract noun: vapor   card   egg   joy   love   peace

H. Directions: Circle any common noun: JOE HAND RABBIT CO ISLE ISLAND

I. Directions: Circle any linking verb: to feel   to skip   to bring   to remain   to be

J. Directions: Write the seven adverbs that tell *to what extent*. _____

_____

K. Directions: Circle any proper adjective: a blue pen   a Swiss knife   a hat brim
258

L. Directions: Circle any adverbs.

Suggestion: Cross out any prepositional phrase(s). However, check to see if any adverb telling **to what extent** is in any prepositional phrase. If it is, circle it. Then, underline the subject once and verb/verb phrase twice. Next, go through the sentence looking specifically for any adverbs that tell **how**. Reread the sentence, searching for any adverbs that tell **when**. Next, look for any adverbs that tell **where**. Finally, look for any adverbs that tell **to what extent** and are not located in a prepositional phrase. This process may sound long, but once you do it step-by-step, it will become faster and will definitely help you to determine adverbs.

1. I can't stay long anyway.

2. Yesterday, the barn was suddenly struck by a very large bolt of lightning.

3. We shall probably arrive quite late.

4. You may not go home yet.

M. Directions: Write the correct possessive form.

1. a pond belonging to Phyllis_____

2. a bone that their dog has - _____

3. many experiences shared by the two boys - _____

4. the ceiling in a kitchen - _____

5. a meadow belonging to more than one goose - _____

N. Directions: Circle any adjectives.

1. African daisies had been planted in several flower beds.

2. Candy's baseball hat with the wide brim is very dirty.

3. That unusual tree in our front yard has tiny pink blossoms.

O. Directions: Fill in the blank.

1. **Wow!   We're winning!**   What part of speech is <u>Wow!</u>? _____

2. **Kay Lynn should have arrived by now.** The main verb is _____.

P. Directions: Cross out any prepositional phrases. Underline the subject once and the verb/verb phrase twice. In the space provided, write the tense: *present, past, future, present perfect, past perfect, future perfect, present progressive, past progressive,* or *future progressive.*

1. _____   Rebecca is planning a surprise party.

2. _____   Have you seen the low clouds on that mountain?

3. _____   Will you finish this within five minutes?

4. _____   He has flown in a helicopter three times.

5. _____   That judge listens carefully to all testimony.

Q. Directions: Underline the subject once and the verb/verb phrase twice. Write P if the group of words is a phrase; write C if the group of words is a clause.

1. _____   Beside the stream.

2. _____   When you finish with that chore.

3. _____   His motorcycle needs a new light.

4. _____   Standing at the edge of the road.

R. Directions: Circle the correct adjective form.

1. His big toe is (smaller, smallest) than his second one.

2. Jennifer thinks that England is (more colorful, most colorful) country of all Europe.

3. Mrs. Elder is the (friendlier, friendliest) Sunday school teacher.

S. Directions: Cross out any prepositional phrases. Underline the subject once and the verb/verb phrase twice. Write D.O. above a word that serves as a direct object; write I.O. above a word that serves as an indirect object.

1. The clown with the red cheeks handed a balloon to the smiling child.

2. Mr. Hansen laughed and handed me a large bag of groceries.

260

T. Directions: Write <u>N</u> if the boldfaced word serves as a noun. Write <u>A</u> if the bold-faced word serves as an adjective. Write <u>V</u> if the boldfaced word serves as a verb.

1. _____   This **fall** they will go to the New England states.

2. _____   The shoppers were all looking for a new **fall** wardrobe.

3. _____   Did you **fall** over the toys scattered on the floor?

4. _____   Mrs. Kent suffered a bad **fall** recently.

U.   Directions: Write the past participle form.

1. to give - _____

2. to write - _____

3. to sing - _____

4. to take - _____

5. to freeze - _____

6. to go - _____

7. to lie - _____

8. to steal - _____

9. to see - _____

10. to lay - _____

11. to fly - _____

12. to bring - _____

13. to swear - _____

14. to come - _____

15. to do - _____

16. to spring - _____

V. Directions: Cross out any prepositional phrases. Underline the subject once and the verb/verb phrase twice.

1. After the beginning of the game, several spectators came in and sat down near the team.

2. Please applaud loudly for this outstanding performer.

3. Many of the zoo animals did not come out of their homes during the rain.

4. Will you go with Mary and me to the symphony tomorrow?

5. The cheerleader jumped excitedly and touched her toes.

W. Directions: Cross out any prepositional phrases. Underline the subject once and the verb/verb phrase twice. On the line provided, write <u>A</u> if the verb is action; write <u>L</u> if the verb is linking.

Suggestion: Write *is, am, are, was,* or *were* above each verb to help you decide.

1. _____ That spaniel seems alert.

2. _____ During the morning hours, we split wood for the fire.

3. _____ This hot cereal tastes too bland without brown sugar.

4. _____ The mother felt the head of her sick son.

X. Directions: Cross out any prepositional phrases. Underline the subject once and the verb/verb phrase twice. Label any predicate nominative-<u>PN</u> Write the proof on the line.

1. A famous composer from Austria was Mozart.

   Proof: _____

2. His new item for his art studio is a large table with a tilted top.

   Proof: _____

Y. Directions: Cross out prepositional phrases. Underline the subject once and the verb/verb phrase twice.

1. Hornets (swarm, swarms) in that area.

2. Magazines (is, are) on the table in the family room.

3. Someone must have (did, done) my job.

4. Has Earl ever (ridden, rode) five miles on a motor scooter?

5. The girls (lay, laid) on their bunks for an afternoon nap.

6. One of the ducks (waddle, waddles) around the lake.

7. Several conference attendees (want, wants) to tour the city.

262

Z.   Directions: Select the correct adverb form.

1. Of the two cars, this one goes (faster, fastest).

2. She can swim underwater (more easily, most easily) than on the surface.

3. At the batting cages, Jonathan hit the fourth ball (harder, hardest).

4. Jane runs (weller, better) after a good night's sleep.

5. Of the triplets, Faith talks (more loudly, most loudly).

AA.   Directions: Fill in the blank.

1. The three determining (limiting) articles are _____, _____, and _____.

2. The four demonstratives that may help you to determine nouns are _____, _____, _____, and _____.

3. The possessive pronouns (used as adjectives) that help locate nouns are _____, _____, _____, _____, _____, _____, and _____.

4. Write an example of a number used as a determining adjective. _____

5. Write an example of a possessive noun used to determine another noun _____
_____

6. Write an indefinite with a noun. _____

BB.   Directions: Write <u>A</u> if the boldfaced word serves as an adjective.   Write <u>P</u> if the boldfaced word serves as a pronoun (stands alone).   Write the adjective and the noun on the line after any sentence marked <u>A</u>.

1. _____ **Few** fireworks were set off during the Fourth of July. _____

2. _____ **Few** were sitting in the back row. _____

3. _____ I want **that** for my collection. _____

4. _____ Who gave you **that** hat? _____

CC.   Directions: Box any nouns.

1. Martha ate three blueberry pancakes, some bacon, and an egg for her breakfast.

2. Has Henry's older brother given you those shoes with the black stripes?

3. Several team members played basketball in that arena during a rainy afternoon.

PUNCTUATION

PERIOD: <u>Rule 1</u>: **Use a period at the end of a declarative sentence (statement).**

I like snow cones.

<u>Rule 2</u>: **Place a period at the end of an imperative sentence (command).**
Pass the salt.

<u>Rule 3</u>: **Use a period after initial(s).**

David James Sloan = David J. Sloan or D. J. Sloan
Lisa Marie Fry = L. M. F.

If a sentence ends with an abbreviation and a period, do not add another period.

<u>Rule 4</u>: **Use a period after the letter(s) and number(s) of an outline.**

I. Civil War
  A. Union
     1. Generals
     2. Strategy
  B. Confederacy
     1. Generals
        a. Robert E. Lee
        b. Thomas "Stonewall" Jackson
     2. Strategy
II. Reconstruction

<u>Rule 5</u>: **Place a period after an abbreviation.**
A. **Days of the week**:

Monday - Mon.	Friday - Fri.
Tuesday - Tues.	Saturday - Sat.
Wednesday - Wed.	Sunday - Sun.
Thursday - Thurs.	

B. **Months of the year**:

January - Jan.	July
February - Feb.	August - Aug.
March - Mar.	September - Sept.
April	October - Oct.
May	November - Nov.
June	December - Dec.

PERIOD: Rule 5:   **Place a period after an abbreviation.***

C. **Times**:

A. M. - (Latin, ante meridiem)   before noon
P. M. - (Latin, post meridiem)   after noon

D. **Directions**:

N. - North   S.W. or SW. - Southwest
S. - South   S.E. or SE. - Southeast
E. - East   N.E. or NE. - Northeast
W. - West   N.W. or NW. - Northwest

E. **Titles**:

Dr. - Doctor   Pres. - President
Mr. - Mister   Sen. - Senator
Mrs. - Mistress   Rep. - Representative
Lieut. - Lieutenant   Prof. - Professor
Capt. - Captain   Gen. - General

F. **Places** (General):

St. - Street   Dr. - Drive
Rd. - Road   Riv. - River
Ave. - Avenue   Mts. - Mountains
Blvd. - Boulevard   Str. - Strait

G. **Places** (Specific):

N.Y. - New York*   U.S. - United States
Med. Sea - Mediterranean Sea St. Paul - Saint Paul

***Do not, however, punctuate postal codes (NY).**

H. **Associations and Organizations**:

A. M. A. - American Medical Association
Y. M. C. A. - Young Men's Christian Association
NOW - National Organization of Women*

*If the name of the organization is an acronym, no
period is used. (An acronym spells out a word.)

I. Others:

Co. - Company   Bldg. - Building
Am. Rev. - American Revolution   yd. - yard*

***Metric measurements do not use a period (cm).**

***Note: Check a dictionary to determine proper abbreviation and use of a
period.** This can be tricky. For example, SA is Seaman Apprentice; S. A. is
South America, South Africa, South Australia, or Salvation Army.

Directions: Insert needed periods.

1.   It's raining today

2.   Please give me your paper

3.   Miss R E Talley has arrived

4.   I Birds

 A Types

 B Care

 II Alligators

 A Types

 B Dangers

5.   The address is 354 W Andrew Lane

6.   Is your tour scheduled for Sept or Nov ?

7.   The Bering Str is located west of Alaska

8.   Do you want to leave Sun or Mon for L A , Calif ?

9.   Was the Stone Age B C or A D ?

10.   At 6 o'clock P M , Capt John Yust arrived on the U S S Independence

11.   Dr Angelic Stomb spoke at an A M A meeting in N Y last May

12.   The Rocky Mts are west of the Miss Riv

13.   During the War of 1812, neither Brit nor Am won

14.   On Fri , Oct 23, Prof Flang will meet with you

15.   The A I Ritter Co has moved to 2435 N Orange Dr , Phx, Arizona

Directions: Insert needed periods.

1.   Our friend will take us down the Hudson Riv and around N Y Harbor on his new

      boat

2.   On Thurs , Mar 5, the members of the Y M C A are invited to a picnic at 9 A M

3.   We live at 6777 S Madison Ave , St Louis, Mo , during the summer

4.   I   Furniture

         A   Antique

             1   Periods

             2   Types

         B   Modern

             1   Periods

             2   Types

5.   The Alps Mts are mountains in Eur that run from France through Switz

6.   Lieut Martha Woods wants to move to Brattleboro, Vt , in a few years

7.   Go west on McGrew Blvd until you come to the International Bldg on the corner

      of McGrew and N 51st Ave in St Paul

8.   Dr and Mrs T L Lewis will visit Den and Czech in the spring

9.   He was approx fifty-six years old on Fri , Apr 11, 1990

APOSTROPHE: Rule 1: **Use an apostrophe in a contraction to show where letter(s) have been omitted.**

can't = cannot
she'll = she will
I've = I have

Rule 2: **Use an apostrophe when the first two digits are omitted from the year.**

'84 = 1984
'99 = 1999

Rule 3: **Use an apostrophe when taking letters or words out of context.** (They will also be underlined.)

You need to cross your t's.
There are too many well's in this paragraph.

Rule 4: **Use an apostrophe to show possession.**

A. **If the word is singular (one), add apostrophe + s ('s).**

barber's chair
blender's buttons
Chris's boots

B. **If the word is plural and ends in s, add the apostrophe after the s (s').**

dogs' kennel
pilots' association
ladies' club

C. **If the word is plural and does NOT end in s, add apostrophe + s ('s).**

women's magazine
oxen's master
children's playground

Note: If two people own something jointly, place the apostrophe after the last person's name.

Joan and Dave's new car

If two people each own items, place the apostrophe after both names.

Bob's and Hannah's new cars

268

Directions: Insert needed apostrophes.

1.   Didnt you want this magazine?

2.   Our swimmers club meets every Thursday.

3.   Those ten cows watering trough doesnt have enough compartments.

4.   Theyll see you in San Diego.

5.   The two boys bedroom was a mess.

6.   Your <u>3s</u> look like <u>8s</u>.

7.   Billys hair is very unmanageable.

8.   Couldnt he open the jar?

9.   I like Tom and Alices stories.

10.   Some of your <u>ands</u> should be replaced with <u>buts</u>.

11.   The street isnt paved yet.

12.   One boys answers were written in ink.

13.   You have forgotten to cross your <u>ts</u>.

14.   Mr. Greenley shouldnt have spoken so crossly to Susans brother.

15.   Their teachers lounge was enlarged last summer.

Directions: Insert needed apostrophes.

1.   Wont you graduate in 96?

2.   Glendas dog cant walk well.

3.   Our ladies meeting wasnt scheduled until Monday.

4.   You have too many <u>buts</u> in the last paragraph.

5.   Our mices tails have strange kinks in them.

6.   Dont you think there are many good points in Larrys essays?

7.   Hasnt the schools debating team returned?

8.   Those <u>5s</u> arent in the correct column, Joe.

9.   Jamess car isnt a new one, but its in nice shape.

10.   Wed be happier if we found Mothers keys.

11.   Youll want to insert synonyms for all the <u>smalls</u> in this story.

12.   The childrens playgrounds havent been cleaned in that area.

13.   The lawyers association held its annual meeting last week.

14.   I havent seen too many <u>mys</u> in anyones writing.

15.   An article about our citys freeway system appeared in todays newspaper.

COMMA: **Rule 1:**   **Use a comma to set off a noun of direct address (a person spoken to).**

Louise, come here, please.
Have you gone, Michael?
I want to go, Roy, with your group.

Rule 2:   **Use a comma to set off introductory words.**

No, I haven't seen it.
Well, I've changed my mind.
Yes, the chimes are new.

Rule 3:   **Use a comma to set off interrupters in a sentence.**

The answer, I think, is fifty-four.
This calendar is, in fact, an old one.
However, not all is lost.
These swings, by the way, need to be repaired.

Rule 4:   **Use a comma after the greeting of a friendly letter.**

Dear Karla,
My dearest friend,

Rule 5:   **Use a comma after the closing of any letter.**

Sincerely yours,
Love,

Rule 6:   **Use a comma to set off words or phrases in a series.**

Furniture, linens, toys, and dishes were sold there.
We ran a mile, swam a half mile, and biked a mile.
You may go to the zoo, to the park, or to the carnival.

Rule 7:   **Use a comma to clarify (make clear) a sentence.**

In the night time was extremely important.
In the night, time was extremely important.

Rule 8:   **Use a comma between two or more descriptive adjectives.**

Bright, sparkling stars twinkled in the dark night.

Do not place a comma between the last adjective and the noun or pronoun.

Note: **If one adjective is a color or a limiting adjective, no comma is placed between the two adjectives.**
Example: A white fluffy puppy ran by.

COMMA: Rule 9:   **Use a comma to set off an appositive from the rest of the sentence.**

Ms. Pratt, <u>the bank president</u>, spoke about loans.
The best student is Gregg, <u>the boy in the last row</u>.
We invited Tracy, <u>our best friend</u>, to dinner.

Rule 10:   **Use a comma between a city and state or country.**

Miami, Florida   London, England

Use a comma to separate the parts of an address.

Bill lives at 567 West Lowe Drive, Tulsa, Oklahoma.

If the city and state or country appear in a sentence, also place a comma after the state or country.

Have you been to Richmond, Virginia, in the fall?
Dallas, Texas, is a growing city.
I moved from 23 Dray Lane, Yuma, Arizona, last fall.

Rule 11:   **Use a comma after a month and year or day and year in a date.**

February, 1980   Jan. 1, 1900

Use a comma after the day of the week if the day appears with the date.

Monday, August 3   Friday, Nov. 7, 1999

If the month and year, or day and year, appear in a sentence, also place a comma after the year.

On June 22, 1898, her grandparents were married.

Rule 12:   **Use a comma at the end of most direct quotations.**

"I would like a hamburger," Gloria said.

If the person who is making the statement is given first, place a comma after the person's name + the verb that follows it.
Gloria said, "I would like a hamburger."

In a split quotation, place a comma after the first part of the quotation and also after the person + the verb (verb + person).
"I agree," replied Mark, "that this rocket is ready."

272

COMMA: Rule 13: **Use a comma to set off a title following a name.**

Gloria Kole, <u>D.D.S.</u>, is opening a new office.
Linn Holter, <u>R.N.</u>, works at Friedland Hospital.

Rule 14: **Use a comma to invert a name.**

<u>Dickinson, Emily</u> is a famous poet.
His name appeared alphabetically as <u>Sween, Guy</u>.

Rule 15: **Use a comma after a dependent clause at the beginning of a sentence.***

<u>After we ate lunch,</u> we went to a movie.
(Dependent Clause)   (Independent Clause)

<u>If I could be there,</u> I would be delighted.
(Dependent Clause)   (Independent Clause)

If the dependent clause is at the end of a sentence, no comma is needed.
We went to a movie after we ate lunch.
I would be delighted if I could be there.

Rule 16: **Use a comma before the conjunction that joins two independent clauses (compound sentence).**

Our outing was fun, but we were glad to return.
(Independent clause)   (independent clause)

Dad cooked dinner, and I set the table.
(Independent clause)   (Independent clause)

Rule 17: **Use a comma after two introductory prepositional phrases or after a long prepositional phrase when a subject follows it.**
In the middle of the night, <u>Frank</u> boarded a plane for Japan.
During the long intermission, <u>everyone</u> chatted.

Rule 18: **Use a comma after an introductory participial phrase.**

<u>Jumping on the bed,</u> the toddler giggled with delight.
<u>Torn into shreds,</u> the red handkerchief hung limply from the bush.

Rule 19: **Use a comma to set off adjectives in apposition.**

<u>Bright and shiny,</u> the gem sparkled in the light.
The gem, <u>bright and shiny,</u> sparkled in the light.

273

Directions: Insert needed commas.

1.   In Rome Italy there are many beautiful fountains.

2.   His entire outlook it seemed had changed.

3.   Miss Ish my kitten has gone to sleep.

4.   Will you help me Kristin?

5.   Yes we will take Route 91 to the caverns.

6.   Dear Matilda

   I am still your friend.

         Love

         Holly

7.   Blue shimmering lights reflected on the lovely calm lake.

8.   During the night owls sat in the barn.

9.   Our address is 27 Haven Avenue Boston Massachusetts.

10.   If you become a famous star remember the folks back home.

11.   They were both born on March 3 1971.

12.   Carl plans on going to Yellowstone and I am going to Yosemite.

13.   She said "Mother may I have some money?"

14.   "I don't have any "   replied Mother.

15.   "With that in mind" she remarked "I'll just stay home."

16.   Sands Mary appeared on the application.

17.   David Smith Ph.D. has written a new book.

18.   The turkeys ducks and chickens have not been fed.

19.   Houston Texas is one of the fastest growing cities in America.

20.   I took a shower brushed my teeth and crawled into bed to read.

Directions: Insert needed commas.

1.   When the medication was too strong she broke out in hives.

2.   Dear Mrs. Gunther

    I will see you on Friday June 10 1999.

            Truly yours
            Fran Mills

3.   The attendant screamed "Get back!"

4.   Large neon letters flashed on the new sign.

5.   On January 1 1980 I was in Chicago Illinois on business.

6.   Rhonda will you paint that wall put new tile in the bathroom and wallpaper the entry?

7.   The knee bruised and bleeding needed immediate attention.

8.   Well those oil derricks in fact have been operating since last summer.

9.   Priscilla cooked pancakes and everyone ate them.

10.   Rose Trost my grandmother was married in Tulsa Oklahoma by a local minister.

11.   The catcher the third base person and the pitcher are up to bat.

12.   This player piano for example is damaged and old but it's very valuable.

13.   The following items are needed for the party: napkins candles and paper plates.

14.   They had to work late but they received a bonus for it.

15.   "Put these clothes " the housekeeper said "in your closet."

16.   If you can't go give me a call Sarah.

17.   Broken off at the base the fountain no longer circulates water.

Directions: Insert needed commas.

1.   Trisha have you met Meryln Jones my dance instructor?

2.   We are still going but we won't leave until tomorrow.

3.   A stained cotton shirt is soaking in a prewash solution.

4.   The fashion artist has been at her new address of 2109 North 10th Street Denver

Colorado since August 23 1982.

5.   The fourth fifth and sixth graders will see a film today.

6.   These canisters for example are sturdier than those.

7.   No my niece from Buffalo New York did not attend Harvard College.

8.   I wasn't there on July 4 1984 in the afternoon.

9.   "The circus is coming to town " said the child.

10.   When you finish with that letter do you want to play chess?

11.   James Russelman D.D.S. has an office in Sacramento California.

12.   "Our major goal" the president of the company said "is to expand."

13.   On September 30 1990 they went to Hawaii Singapore and New Zealand.

14.   The expensive pants however fell apart after the first washing.

15.   Her name appeared on the list as Martin Cynthia Ann.

16.   His cheeks red and glowing appeared very swollen.

17.   Standing in a grocery line the lady thumbed through several magazines.

18.   After the long drought during the summer rain fell steadily for four days.

SEMICOLON: Rule 1: **Use a semicolon (;) to join two independent clauses that are closely related.**

The rain stopped; the sun came out.
(independent clause)   (independent clause)

His voice was too soft; we couldn't hear him.
(independent clause)   (independent clause)

Do not place _and_, _but_, or _or_ after a semicolon.

Incorrect: This scarf is pretty; and I might buy it for my sister.

Correct: This scarf is pretty; I might buy it for my sister.

If a word such as _therefore_ or _however_ appears after the semicolon, place a comma after it.

You may go out to play; however, you must wear a jacket.

COLON: Rule 1: **Use a colon after the greeting of a business letter.**

Gentlemen:
Dear Mrs. Rinehart:

Rule 2: **Use a colon in writing the time.**

9:00 A.M.
11:23 P.M.

Rule 3: **Use a colon to set off lists.**

Groceries:
milk
bread
cookies

The following people must attend: Val, Sue, and Ty.

Rule 4: **Use a colon between the chapter and verse(s) in the _Bible_.**
John 3:16
Genesis 7: 1-11

Rule 5: **Use a colon after divisions of topics in a writing.**

COMMAS: Rule 1:
Rule 2:

277

Name_____

Date_____

Directions: Insert needed colons and semicolons.

1.   Marge emptied the trash Jim set the table.

2.   It's now 530 P.M.

3.   We need the following items sugar, milk, and eggs.

4.   Have you ever read Galatians 4 23-25 in the <u>Bible</u>?

5.   Dear Sir

    Please send me three copies of your magazine, <u>Signs of the Times</u>.

                Sincerely yours,
                Bill Stout

6.   Rule A Do not pick any flowers.

    Rule B Stay off the grass.

7.   At 900 A.M. we ordered the following 2 chairs, a table, and three lamps.

8.   We turned in our <u>Bible</u> to Matthew 6 2-9.

9.   I want to go please wait for me.

10.   Gentlemen and Ladies of the Board

    I wish to address the problem of several ineffective computers. May I meet with you on Tuesday, July 4th, at 1130 A.M.?

                Best wishes,
                Annette J. Bevins

11.   The game has gone into overtime however, I think our team will win.

12.   Things to do
   -Clean room
   -Take out trash

| **QUESTION MARK:** | Rule: | **Use a question mark at the end of an interrogative sentence.** |

Does her niece live in Kansas.
Have you ever ridden a bull?

| **EXCLAMATION POINT:** | Rule 1: | **Use an exclamation point after an exclamatory sentence (one showing strong feeling).** |

Look out!
We won!

| | Rule 2: | **Use an exclamation point after a word or phrase that shows strong feeling (interjection).** |

Yeah! You did it!
Good grief! Someone ate my lunch!

| **HYPHEN:** | Rule 1: | **Place a hyphen between fractions and certain numbers.** |

two-fifths
three-fourths
twenty-one
seventy-seven

| | Rule 2: | **Use a hyphen when dividing a word of two or more syllables at the end of a line. (You must have at least two letters on the first line and three on the following line.)** |

_____un-
happy_____
_____wonder-
ful_____

| | Rule 3: | **Use a hyphen to combine some prefixes with abase word.** |

ex-president   self-rising

Check a **dictionary** to determine if a word is hyphenated.

HYPHEN: <u>Rule 4</u>: **Use a hyphen to combine some closely related words.**

two-handed
to-and-fro

Check a dictionary to determine if a word should be hyphenated.

<u>UNDERLINING</u>:

<u>Rule 1</u>: **Underline the names of ships, planes, and trains.**

Do you like the <u>Spirit of St. Louis</u>?
The <u>Silverton Express</u> arrives at nine o'clock.
The <u>U.S.S. Constitution</u> is in Boston Harbor.*

*This may also be written **U.S.S.** <u>Constitution</u>.

<u>Rule 2</u>: **Underline letter(s), word(s), or numeral(s) used out of context.**

You forgot to dot your <u>i</u>!
This sentence has too many <u>and's</u>.
A <u>7</u> should appear in the first column.

<u>Rule 3</u>: **Underline the title of books, magazines, movies, newspapers, plays, television shows, record albums, CD's, tapes, long stories, and works of art.**

Have you read the book, <u>Tex</u>?
I like the magazine entitled <u>Field and Stream</u>.
The old movie, <u>Lassie Come Home</u>, is interesting.
Is <u>The Wall Street Journal</u> delivered daily?
The play, <u>Annie Get Your Gun</u>, was amusing.
Many children enjoyed Oscar on <u>Sesame Street</u>, the television show.
Your tape, <u>In His Time</u>, has finished playing.

<u>Rule 4</u>: **In printed materials, any item that should be underlined can be in italics.**

The child's father read <u>My Mother Doesn't Like to Cook</u> at bedtime.

or

The child's father read *My Mother Doesn't Like to Cook* at bedtime.

280

PUNCTUATION
Question Marks
Exclamation Marks
Hyphens
Underlinings

Directions: Insert needed punctuation (question marks, exclamation marks, hyphens, and underlinings).

1. Wow   I won the first prize in archery

2. Did you barbecue the chicken

3. Three fourths of the messages were unimportant.

4. We were given a three pronged fork for the job.

5. Have you ever sailed on the ship, Princess

6. The ex chief of police had sailed on the Titanic.

7. Rats I forgot to include my address on the envelope

8. When I was twenty one, I went aboard the Queen Mary.

9. The ex marine worked for thirty years as a professional bor
    der patrol.

10. Have you seen the movie, Gone with the Wind, or read the book, Susannah

11. He lives in a tri level that includes seventy four units.

12. The newspaper, The Penny Stock Journal, interests many people, especially busi
     ness people.

13. Have you seen the movie, Fiddler on the Roof, or the television series, Alice

14. The Axter family hasn't seen the play, Oklahoma, for several years.

15. Did you know that Clark Jones was a self educated man who, in fact, de
     veloped a new style of shoe.

QUOTATION MARKS:

Rule 1:   **Use some quotation marks (" ") to indicate someone's exact word or words.**

"Are the baseball hats here?" asked Hannah.
Tom said, "Let's go for pizza."

A. **In a split quotation, use quotation marks around each part spoken.**

"I see," said Blake, "that you drive."
"Jean knows," said the man, "your idea."

B. **In a quotation that is not split, do not place the ending quotation mark until speaker is finished. This may involve many sentences.**

"Don't talk. Look at me." said Kelly.

C. **In dialogue, each time a person speaks, a new paragraph is begun.**

"I like the mountains of Vermont," Milly remarked.
Thelma replied, "Let's go there next winter."
"I can't," said Milly, "because I'm going to England then."

Note: If the entire sentence is a quotation, place the end punctuation inside the final quotation mark.

The instructor asked, "Did you try?"

If the entire sentence is not a quotation, place a period or comma inside the quotation mark. All other punctuation is placed outside the quotation mark.

I read the article, "Pain."

Rule 2:   **Use quotation marks to enclose the titles of chapters, articles, poems, essays, short stories, nursery rhymes, and songs.**

I like Kipling's poem entitled "If."
Many read "Dear Abby" in the daily paper.

Note: **Any "Item" that is contained within a larger one is usually placed in quotation marks. Chapters are in a book. Articles are in newspapers and magazines.**

Directions: Insert needed quotation marks.

1. Barry said,   Hello. How are you?

2. Our butler replied to the remark,   How dreadful for you.

3. Who is studying for the exam?   asked Barbara.

4. Donna exclaimed,   I love snow!

5. Has the baby sitter read Little Red Riding Hood to the children?

6. Is this,   asked Jean,   the comb that you want?

7. Yankee Doodle was a popular song during the American Revolution.

8. Wilma exclaimed,   I can't believe that we are finally here!

9. I love the poem, Death of a Hired Man.

10. I rapidly read the assigned chapter, Reconstruction, in my American history class, and then enjoyed the magazine article entitled What Is Your IQ? in a psychology periodical.

11. Don't light the candle,   he ordered,   or you will regret it.

12. These records,   Macy replied,   are current ones.

13. Have you ever read the funny story, Thirteen?

14. Stay here,   Kent replied,   and I'll go to get help.

15. Peg said that her cat was taken to a veterinarian.

Directions: Insert needed quotation marks.

1.   Sam asked,   Which way is it to the tropical gardens?

2.   Dad enjoys the newspaper article entitled Food.

3.   Were you,   asked the detective,   at the Hand's house on the night of the incident?

4.   Most people have read the nursery rhyme,   Jack and Jill.

5.   Father shouted,   Come back!   You forgot your luggage!

6.   The story,   Cat and the Underworld,   is interesting.

7.   Who,   the unhappy customer asked,   is in charge here?

8.   Did you enjoy the chapter entitled Living Things?

9.   Your picture is crooked,   said Valerie.

10.   Down in the Valley is an unusual melody.

11.   The lost hikers screamed,   We're over here!

12.   One of Ralph Waldo Emerson's poems is entitled We Thank Thee.

13.   Some of these,   remarked Theda,   have already been eaten.

14.   We clipped the magazine article,   Secrets of a Coupon Saver.

15.   Tiffany asked,   Did you read the article about crime in today's newspaper?

Directions: Use quotation marks or underlining as needed.

1.   the short story, Cat and the Underworld

2.   the poem, Why Nobody Pets the Lion at the Zoo

3.   the movie, Raiders of the Lost Ark

4.   the play, Annie

5.   the chapter, Living Things

6.   the book, Summer of the Monkeys

7.   the television show, Price Is Right

8.   the essay, Land of Opportunity

9.   the ship, Queen Mary

10.   the newspaper, Washington Post

11.   the airplane, Concorde

12.   the magazine, Better Homes and Gardens

13.   the magazine article, Sweet Revenge

14.   the newspaper article, Dealing with Life

15.   the train, Orient Express

16.   the nursery rhyme, Humpty Dumpty

17.   the song, How Great Thou Art

18.   the album, Pictures at Eleven

19.   the painting, Mona Lisa

20.   the book, Autobiography of My Mother

Name_____

Date_____

Directions: Use quotation marks or underlining as needed.

1.   the magazine, People

2.   the television show, Electric Company

3.   the poem, Dust

4.   the movie, Apple Dumpling Game

5.   the newspaper, Gettysburg Times

6.   the ship, U. S. S. Arizona

7.   the newspaper article, Women in the News

8.   the essay, The Significance of Education

9.   the book, Cat Ate My Gym Suit

10.   the song, Jingle Bells

11.   the book, Rumble Fish

12.   the airplalne, Spruce Goose

13.   the nursery rhyme, Hickory Dickory Dock

14.   the magazine article, Let's Go Roller Skating

15.   the play, Cat on a Hot Tin Roof

16.   the chapter, Your Body

17.   the painting, Sunday Best

18.   the book, Crafty Bazaar Gifts

19.   the poem, I Knew You Once

20.   the short story, Thirteen

Name_____ **PUNCTUATION**

Date_____

Directions: Insert needed punctuation.

1.   Do you enjoy reading magazines like Redbook or books like Blubber

2.   The U S S Arizona sank Dec 7 1941 at eight oclock in the morning that was
     Japans attack on Pearl Harbor Hawaii

3.   5638 E Crenter Blvd
                                          Arlington Virginia
                                          Mar 4 20--

     My dearest Aunt Joy
            Have you seen the play entitled Music Man   Wouldn't it be great
     to see that play visit the Spruce Goose* and fly to London England for a
     few weeks

                                          Love
                                          Netty

4.   When you write minister in that sentence capitalize the m

5.   I havent any money but I want to go to Martin Shoe Stores sale

6.   Grip Enterprises
     4554 Libby St
     Amarillo Texas

     Dear Sir
            Ill be visiting your office on Monday Sept 9 and I hope you can
     spare a few minutes

                                          Sincerely yours
                                          R H Durango

7.   Waiting for a bus the young man read for a few minutes stared at passing cars
     and drifted off to sleep

        *name of an airplane

Name_____

Date_____

Directions: Insert needed punctuation.

1.   A large red truck just passed us Sarah

2.   Dot your i in this word and your paper will be perfect

3.   Charity likes to dance most of us would rather sit and watch

4.   We passed a meadow a brook and a run down mill

5.   Greta Tarkin her sister in law cant visit Memphis Tennessee in June

6.   Although the children's library is five blocks away well go there

7.   Marsha asked Where is the Grand Canyon

8.   Have you seen asked the sales lady our new line of carpeting

9.   Ive always wanted to read the book entitled Megatrends and to see Shakespeares play Romeo and Juliet

10.   Dear Lucy

        Youre the best friend in the world we get along well

                        Your friend
                        Meggin

11.   Her eyes red and swollen looked somewhat bloodshot

12.   The article entitled Speaker of the House in the magazine Good Housekeeping was interesting

13.   The giraffes lions tigers and gorillas were the most interesting

14.   I read a novel and Marty sang the song entitled Bicycle Built for Two

15.   May I asked Mr Anderson the real estate agent help you sell your home

Name_____

Date_____

Directions: Insert needed punctuation.

1.   Because the door was locked we couldnt enter Pauls home

2.   Marie said Grandma youre so nice to me

3.   It was a bright striped scarf that was given to A J Snead the retiring librarian

4.   Our girls locker room isnt on this floor

5.   Were going tomorrow and you will come next week

6.   Your ts need to be crossed otherwise everything in the essay is correct Heidi

7.   Our plumber Tracy Smith works long hard hours   said Jeanette

8.   Derrick isnt my brother my brothers name is Ralph

9.   No Janet the post office address is not 46 Barrow Lane Cheyenne Wyoming

10.   There were three selected for the team Janice Sam and Andy

11.   It seems said the man quietly that you have made a mistake

12.   Her up to date ideas earned her a job with Targon Co St Louis Mo

13.   One fourth of the animals hadnt been given the vaccine prepared by Dr Sturks our local veterinarian

14.   The completion date will be August 24 2057 at 5 00 P M

15.   Youre without a doubt one of our groups best swimmers Ruth

Name_____ **PUNCTUATION**

Date_____

Directions: Insert needed punctuation.

1.   The R E Polk Co opened a new office at 17842 N Andrews Ave Greensburg Pa

2.   One third of Daryls class had visited Seattle Washington at some time

3.   On Tuesday Feb 7 1904 my father was born in Prescott Arizona

4.   Mary have you seen this childs purple sweater

5.   Wow Our team in fact scored thirty nine points

6.   Yes we are going aboard the Queen Mary* on Friday Oct 6th

7.   Mr and Mrs Hahn please send me the following three pencils six rulers and a box of crayons

8.   Joan asked Whos that

9.   322 Deflin St
                                                 Birmingham Alabama
                                                 Mar 4 1957

       Dear Dorothy

              Im enclosing twenty one pictures of my familys vacation

                                                 Love
                                                 Sandy

10.   This day said Gloria is the greatest

11.   No there arent too many alsos in your first paragraph

12.   Gentlemen

              The first board meeting was held June 2 1993 at 2 00 P M in Chicago Illinois

                                                 Respectfully submitted

                                                 Wayne P Coles

*name of a ship

CAPITALIZATION

Rule 1:   **Capitalize the first letter of the first word in a sentence.**

      Example: **P**earls are very elegant.

Rule 2:   **Capitalize the pronoun I.**

      Example: Had the captain forgotten that **I** left early?

Rule 3:   **Capitalize the first letter of the first word in most lines of poetry.**

      Example: **W**hose woods these are I think I know

If the words of a line of poetry will not fit on one line, indent the next line and continue writing. However, do not capitalize the first word of the continuing line.

      Example: <u>**W**hose woods these are I</u>
                         <u> think I know   </u>

Rule 4:   **Capitalize the first word, the last word, and all important words in any title.**

      Do not capitalize <u>a</u>, <u>an</u>, <u>the</u>, <u>and</u>, <u>but</u>, <u>or</u>, <u>nor</u>, or prepositions of four or less letters unless located as the first or last word of a title. CAPITALIZE ALL OTHER WORDS IN A TITLE.

         A.   **Always capitalize verbs.**
               Example: <u>**E**ight **Is E**nough</u>

         B.   **Capitalize prepositions of five or more letters.**
               Example: "**D**on't **S**it **U**nder the **A**pple **T**ree"

Rule 5:   **Capitalize Roman numerals and the letters for the first major topics in an outline. Capitalize the first letter of the first word in in an outline.**

         I.   Energy
            A. Types
               1.   **P**hysical
               2.   **N**uclear
            B. **V**arious uses
        II.   **M**atter

Name_____   **CAPITALIZATION**

Date_____

Directions: Supply needed capitalization.

1.   has anyone seen the movie, <u>mustang country</u>?

2.   did i give you "jack and the beanstalk" to read?

3.   i. fight for independence

      a. battles

      b. important people

  ii. battle of 1812

      a. events

      b. historical significance

4.   the movie, <u>snoopy comes home</u>, was playing at a local theater.

5.   he and i don't know where to find <u>the witch tree symbol</u> on the shelves.

6.   the poem began, "today, a red-breasted robin sat upon my aleppo pine..."

7.   that book entitled <u>the adventure of odysseys and the tale of troy</u> is interesting.

8.   "the donkey" is the name of a poem that begins, "when fishes flew and forests walked..."

9.   have you seen my copy of <u>cowboy songs and other frontier ballads</u>?

10.   this story entitled "every dog should own a man" is one I want to read.

11.   "a bird came down the walk" is a poem by emily dickinson.

12.   we read the action-packed book, <u>first through the grand canyon</u>.

CAPITALIZATION

Rule 6: **Capitalize the first letter of the first word in a direct quotation.**

Examples: Lyle asked, "Where's my comb?"

"In the drawer," replied his father.

In a split quotation, do not capitalize the first letter of the word in the second part unless a new sentence is begun.

Examples: "Did you," asked Joe, "open this door?"

"I'm finished," yelled Chris, "Let's go!"

Rule 7: **Capitalize Mother, Dad, and other titles when they serve as a replacement for the person's name.**

Example: We haven't told Mother about our plan.

You can insert the person's name for <u>Mother</u>; the **M** is capitalized: We haven't told **Mother** (**Debra**) about our plan.

Example: How are you feeling, Son?

You can insert the person's name for <u>Son</u> so the **S** is capitalized: How are you feeling, **Dan**?

Capitalize the title if it appears with a name.

Examples: Grandpa Smith
Aunt Cecilia
Captain Lowe
Judge Worth
Senator Billings
Cousin Lee

Rule 8: **Capitalize the names of organizations.**

Examples: Boy Scouts of America
American Red Cross
Kiwanis Club

Directions: Supply needed capitalization.

1.   my aunt gail belongs to bingham school parent teacher organization.

2.   the child remarked,   "it's hot in here."

3.   the women's world association meets in mayor larkin's office.

4.   "where have you been?"   the upset mother asked.

5.   i asked dad for his car keys.

6.   has councilman barett contacted you, mother?

7.   "this pottery,"   replied the leader,   "was made by alice's nephew."

8.   "do you want to join the welcome wagon club?"   asked ms. partin.

9.   when did grandmother see representative kelly?

10.   my sister has joined the national honor society.

11.   the guest speaker at our 4-h club meeting was corporal jenkins.

12.   roberta jumped and yelled,   "let's go!"

13.   "will you come here, son?"   asked dad.

14.   "may i stay?"   commented harriet,   "there's plenty of room for me."

15.   "your daughter should join the maryland young executives club,"   said martin.

CAPITALIZATION

Rule 9: **Capitalize business names.**

Examples:

Fanton Enterprises	American Airlines
Brown Company	Jolen's Restaurant
Pratt Limited	Fast Body Shop, Inc.
Crenton Inn	Beamer Grocery Store

Rule 10: **Capitalize government bodies and departments.**

Examples:

Senate	Congress
House of Representatives	Cabinet
Department of Interior	Treasury Department

Rule 11: **Capitalize institution names.**

Examples:

Goldton Hospital	Pioneer School
University of Florida	Adams County Jail

Rule 12: **Capitalize names of particular geographic places.**

Examples:

Potomac River	Canada
Andes Mountains	Sunset Point
Lake Superior	Cape Cod
Bering Strait	Tampa Bay
North Sea	Gulf of Mexico
Miller Creek	Carlsbad Caverns
Atlantic Ocean	Meteor Crater
Catalina Island	Mammoth Cave
Great Plains	New England

Rule 13: **Capitalize historical events, periods of time, and historical documents.**

Examples:

Ice Age	American Revolution
Battle of Waterloo	Middle Ages
Magna Carta	Declaration of Independence

Directions: Supply needed capitalization.

1.   from the corner of market street and central avenue, curve around bristol lake until you come to cripton's general store.

2.   last summer they visited yellowstone national park, disneyland, knott's berry farm, and san francisco bay.

3.   the turning point battle of the civil war was at gettysburg, pennsylvania.

4.   the asian hunters crossed the bering strait and traveled through north america.

5.   the cress travel agency made the family's hawaiian islands reservations.

6.   when ed and his family visited washington, d. c., they saw the buildings of the department of education, the famous potomac river, and georgetown university.

7.   our class studied about the house of burgesses and jamestown's early beginnings.

8.   take darkston's limousine service to los angeles international airport to catch your united airline flight to denver, colorado.

9.   our vacation schedule includes the following: niagara falls, the pocono mountains, mt. rushmore, and yosemite national park.

10.   in the morning, we ran errands to hartzel's dry cleaning service and himball department store.

CAPITALIZATION

Rule 14: **Capitalize names of days, months, holidays, and special days.**

Examples: Saturday   Columbus Day

Fourth of July   Hanukkah

December   St. Valentine's Day

Pearl Harbor Day   George Washington's Birthday

February   Tuesday

Rule 15: **Capitalize a proper adjective but not the noun it modifies unless the noun is part of a title.**

Examples: a Columbus Day parade

our Tuesday meeting

Hanukkah celebration

Alaskan coast

Swiss village

Labor Day weekend

a Scottsdale rodeo

Specific titles are capitalized following the rule: Capitalize the first word, the last word, and all important words in any title. Do not capitalize <u>a</u>, <u>an</u>, <u>the</u>, <u>and</u>, <u>but</u>, <u>or</u>, <u>nor</u>, or prepositions of four or less letters unless those words are the first or last word.

Examples: California Gold Rush Days

Washington Cherry Blossom Festival

Pasadena Tournament of Roses Parade

Winter Olympics

Kansas State Fair

Note: Include <u>the</u> in a title only if <u>the</u> actually would appear on a sign announcing the event.

Examples: Are you going to the Orange Bowl Parade?
They went to the Indianapolis 500.

Rule 16: **Capitalize brand names but not the product(s).**

Examples: Roman Meal bread   Carnation milk

Birdseye vegetables   Fisher Price recorder

Directions: Supply needed capitalization.

1. last monday the band marched in a memorial day parade.

2. our family celebrated grandparents' day at an italian restaurant.

3. at our thursday meeting we will plan a st. patrick's day party.

4. most baseball fans know if the world series begins on a sunday.

5. did carl participate in the 1983 marathon sponsored by dole company in hawaii?

6. the purchases included crisco shortening, pampers diapers, kraft grated cheese,

    hormel ham.

7. during friday's storm, signs of the texas state fair fell down.

8. after thanksgiving vacation, the convention will meet in a palm springs hotel.

9. in july we will attend the biglerville chamber of commerce annual music festival.

10. do you know that veteran's day is the same as armistice day?

11. doris and i bought folger's coffee, nabisco shredded wheat, and campbell's

    soup.

12. this christmas vacation we will spend two days at a colorado ski resort near

    denver.

CAPITALIZATION

Rule 17: **Capitalize religions, religious denominations, religious documents, names of churches, and names for a supreme being.**

Examples:

Hindu religion	**P**rotestant
God	**I**slam religion
Dead **S**ea **S**crolls	**T**orah
Methodist	**L**ady of the **V**alley **C**atholic **C**hurch
Heavenly **F**ather	**A**llah
Ten **C**ommandments	**L**utheran

Notes:

A. a **B**aptist church: Capitalize only **B**aptist because a specific name of a church is not given. <u>Baptist</u> is a denomination and should be capitalized.

   Madison **B**aptist **C**hurch: Capitalize the name of a church.

B. Greek or Roman gods and goddesses: Do not capitalize the terms, *gods* and *goddesses*.

   Athena and **Z**eus: Capitalize the names of gods and goddesses.

Rule 18: **Capitalize languages.**

Examples:

English	**G**erman	**L**atin
Spanish	**F**rench	**A**rabic

Rule 19: **Capitalize races and ethnic groups.**

Examples:

Caucasian	**P**olynesian	**H**ispanic
Indian	**N**egro	**C**ajun

Rule 20: **Capitalize North, South, East, West, Northeast, Northwest, Southeast, and Southwest when they refer to a region of the country or the world.**

Examples: Does your Uncle Ray live in the **E**ast?

   The **S**outhwest includes the state of Arizona.

Directions: Supply needed capitalization.

1.   my mother speaks english, italian, and russian.

2.   this basket, made by indians, is of outstanding quality.

3.   the riverdale methodist church hosted a polynesian luau.

4.   in the <u>bible</u> there are references to god's leading the hebrews out of egypt.

5.   a class on hispanic culture will be conducted in both spanish and english.

6.   have they studied the gods and goddesses of greek mythology in literature class?

7.   the franklin family lived in south carolina and in some other state in the south.

8.   has inga, your aunt, learned to speak swedish yet?

9.   the roman catholic faith is dominant in latin america.

10.   that lutheran church located west of my home held a <u>bible</u> school in june.

11.   the hopi indians of the southwest make beautiful jewelry.

12.   do you know anything about the shinto religion of japan?

13.   church services at santiago baptist church are conducted in spanish.

14.   some exchange students studied modern art and chinese at a college in the new england states.

15.   did king david, the great israelite leader, write psalm 100?

CAPITALIZATION

<u>Rule 21</u>: **Capitalize specific names of structures.**

      Examples: **E**mpire **S**tate **B**uilding

                       Golden **G**ate **B**ridge

                       Eiffel **T**ower

                       Washington **M**onument

                       Yankee **S**tadium

                       Astrodome

                       Grand **C**entral **S**tation

<u>Rule 22</u>: **Capitalize names, initials, and titles appearing with names.**

      Examples: **A**be

                       Debra **R**. Stone

                       Professor **E**lik

                       Admiral **J**ames **S**tevens

                       Fido

<u>Rule 23</u>: **Capitalize political parties and their members.**

      Examples: **R**epublican **P**arty

                       Democrats

                       Communist **P**arty

                       Tories

<u>Rule 24</u>: **Capitalize the first letter only in most hyphenated words that begin a sentence.**

      Examples: **T**wenty-two ducks use that pond.

                       Fathers-in-law meet in this room today.

Capitalize both parts of a hyphenated word in titles.

      Examples: Did you know that **V**ice-**P**resident Mondale ran for

                       President?

                       Cindy has memorized the "**T**wenty-**T**hird Psalm."

Rule 25: **Capitalize President when it refers to the leader of the United States.**

Examples: Have you seen that famous portrait of **P**resident George Washington?

The **P**resident has called a press conference.

Rule 26: **Capitalize a specific, well-known area or event.**

Examples: Did President Bush work late in the **O**val **O**ffice?

Her ice skating at the **W**inter **O**lympics was fantastic.

Rule 27: **Capitalize the first word of the greeting and closing of a letter.**

Examples: **D**ear Jane,

My dear and favorite niece,

Karla,

Love,

Sincerely yours,

My very best wishes,

Date_____

Directions: Supply needed capitalization.

1.   does dr. shinley have an office at lincoln medical hospital?

2.   the democratic party held a convention in san francisco, california.

3.   we met captain ted r. yost at the police building on macaroni avenue.

4.   has aunt gloria or dad ever visited sears tower in chicago?

5.   your pictures of lincoln memorial are very clear, beverly.

6.   many of us would like to visit notre dame cathedral in paris, france.

7.   in the country of pakistan, there is a special province called north-west frontier province.

8.   should this road lead to the leaning tower of pisa?

9.   a search is being conducted for sergeant major glugg.

10.   my friend, t. r. franklin, is a stockbroker for that company.

11.   both the lincoln tunnel and the george washington bridge lead into n. y. c.

12.   if you, clarence, favored staying with england during the american revolution, you probably would have belonged to the tory party.

13.   the fiesta bowl is held annually at sun devil stadium.

14.   did you realize that the smithsonian institution has many buildings?

15.   i would have liked to have been a colonist in plymouth when john carver was the governor.

DO NOT CAPITALIZE

Rule 1: **Do not capitalize north, south, east, west, northeast, northwest, southeast and southwest when they are used as directions.**

    Examples: Go north on 57th Street.

                       Do you live east or west of the Mississippi River?

However, capitalize the direction when it appears with a geographic place.

    Examples: The barber lives at 863 **W**est Hooly Drive.

                       Do you live on **S**outh Friar Street?

Rule 2: **Do not capitalize school subjects unless they state a language, or they are numbered.**

    Examples: I enjoy **E**nglish.

                       Is **A**lgebra I meeting here?

                       My favorite subjects are spelling, history, and math.

If a proper adjective appears with the subject, capitalize only the proper adjective.

    Examples: **A**merican history.

                       Greek literature

Rule 3: **Do not capitalize seasons of the year.**

    Examples: spring   winter

                     summer   fall/autumn

Rule 4: **Do not capitalize foods, games, trees, musical instruments, animals, diseases, and plants. If a proper adjective appears with the item, capitalize only the proper adjective.**

FOODS: pizza   ice cream   **S**wedish meatballs

          creamed corn   tuna   **I**talian sauce

	Spanish rice	Swiss cheese	lettuce

GAMES:	chess	bridge	football
	Chinese checkers	tag	Mexican hat dance
	two square	English soccer	polo

However, capitalize the names of trademarked games.
Example: Monopoly

TREES:	oak	ash
	elm	Mexican fan palm
	apple	silk oak

MUSICAL INSTRUMENTS:	piano	drums	harp
	French horn	violin	guitar

DISEASES:	mumps	Hodgkin's disease	chicken pox
	measles	cerebral palsy	flu
	cancer	German measles	Asiatic flu

PLANTS:	tulips	asparagus fern	philodendron
	oleander	Bermuda grass	ice plant
	cactus	American rose	gardenia

ANIMALS:	kitten	poodle	armadillo
	palomino	giraffe	German shepherd
	Siamese cat	snake	Arabian horse
	Asiatic beetle	Clydesdale horse	monkey

Directions: Supply needed capitalization.

1.   the accountant lived in the northern part of south dakota.

2.   a german shepherd dog patrols gorbam industries on delta avenue.

3.   she purchased her saxophone on friday at mernet music store.

4.   last fall melinda took a course in spanish literature.

5.   the rotary club met at gringo's mexican food restaurant and feasted on cheese crisps.

6.   in our front yard, the gardener planted italian cypress, daffodils, chrysanthemums, and japanese anemone.

7.   the doctor's questionnaire requested to know if i had ever had the following: measles, diphtheria, scarlet fever, polio, or hong kong flu.

8.   marvin studies english, economics, american literature, computer science I, and psychology at a western university.

9.   when i had pneumonia last winter, my british friend played backgammon with me.

10.   his favorite foods are greek pie, bologna, onion rings, boston creme pie, and danish pastries.

Date_____

Directions: Supply needed capitalization.

1.   have you read <u>island of the blue dolphins</u>, aunt barbara?

2.   in history, i learned that the <u>u.s. constitution</u> replaced the <u>articles of confederation</u>.

3.   on easter we attended the lion's club fifth annual pancake breakfast held in the social hall of memorial presbyterian church.

4.   did mr. applebee serve sara lee cupcakes or mississippi fudge pie for dessert?

5.   the city of port chester is in southeastern new york on long island sound.

6.   the language of poland is one of the indo-european languages called slavic.

7.   the pets-are-fun shop on milter lane has a siberian husky, various snakes, and two french poodles.

8.
                             45785 w. arms drive
                             reno, nevada
                             august 10, 20--

dear cousin steven,

     we are enjoying the west. yesterday, we visited an arabian horse farm, and on saturday we leave for organ pipe national monument.

                             your friend,

                             clyde

Directions: Supply needed capitalization.

1.   the battle of new orleans at the end of the war of 1812 made general andrew jackson famous.

2.   the laketon wildlife club meets at sunset park restaurant on wednesdays.

3.   the children watched <u>sesame street</u> and then read <u>winnie the pooh and the blustery day</u>.

4.   that brownie troop visited the baltimore museum of art last summer during the third week in july.

5.   lillian asked, "have you planted an american rose in this planter?"

6.   the country of france is bordered by spain, the mediterranean sea, the english channel, belgium, switzerland, italy, luxembourg, and the atlantic ocean.

7.   my father entered general eisenhower hospital on eighth street during christmas vacation.

8.   in the mexican history class, we studied aztec indians and chief montezuma.

9.   our tour of the white house* and our trip to the jefferson memorial were interesting.

10.   the u.s. figure skating association held competitions last summer.

* particular building where the President resides
308

Directions: Supply needed capitalization.

1. most of greenland lies north of the arctic circle and is bordered by the arctic

    ocean.

2. "dad, will you," asked yvonne, "take me to the san diego zoo?"

3. I. literature

        a. prose

        b. poetry

4. is desert sky junior high school near union hills road?

5. the article entitled "three days to the desk of your dreams" appeared in the august

    issue of <u>success</u> magazine.

6.

                                15 north monte cristo drive
                                san clemente, california
                                october 21, 20--

    department of revenue
    p.o. box 333
    augusta, maine

    to whom it may concern:

        enclosed is the information requested.

                                truly yours,

                                w. t. phillips

Name_____

Date_____

Directions: Supply needed capitalization.

1.   last summer we went to a wyoming ranch, a yacht race, and a delaware beach.

2.   has great aunt daisy been to the great wall in china?

3.   the crusades were fought between the christians and the muslims.

4.   send your copyright form to register of copyrights, library of congress, washington, d. c.

5.   before leaving the ship, <u>mayflower,</u> the pilgrims drew up their plan of government called the "mayflower compact."

6.   does carnell department store carry tubas, gloria vanderbilt perfume, or african daisies?

7.   a dinner honoring lieutenant colonel keplinger will be held at snakehorn restaurant next saturday evening.

8.   john ciardi's poem entitled "why nobody pets the lion at the zoo" begins, "the morning that the world began..."

9.   a leukemia patient was transferred to good heart general hospital for further blood tests.

10.   the holland tulip festival is held yearly in michigan.

FRIENDLY LETTER

Parts:

The parts of a friendly letter are the heading, the salutation or greeting, the body, the closing, and the signature.

	Your Post Office Box
	or
	Number and Street Name
heading	City, State Zip Code
	Complete Date

greeting   Dear (Person) ,

_____ The written message in any letter is called **the body**. _____

_____

_____

closing   *Appropriate closing,

signature   Your Name

*The closing/signature should be lined up with the heading.

Note: It has become acceptable to abbreviate the state even in formal letter writing. In using the postal codes, both letters are capitalized and no period is used.

FRIENDLY LETTER

1087 North Main Avenue

Honolulu, Hawaii

October 23, 2089

My dear friend,

Hi! How are you? It's been a long time since I've written so there's so much to ask you. Did you take your planned trip to St. Louis and Washington, D. C.? Did you visit the White House, the Lincoln Memorial, or the Washington Monument? I'm anxious to hear all about your trip.

Our family didn't do much this past summer. Dad started his own business, and we didn't have much extra cash for anything *big*. We did manage to go up to the mountains for some picnics and to the beach often. That's one nice thing about living here.

Speaking of *here*, when do you think your family can visit us? Write and let me know. I miss the good times we had in our old neighborhood.

Love,

Chris

BUSINESS LETTER

Parts:

The parts of a business letter are the heading, the inside address, the salutation or greeting, the body, the closing, and the signature.

                                    Your Post Office Box
                                            or
                                    Number and Street Name

                    heading   City, State   Zip Code

                                    Complete Date

Name of Business

Street Address of Business   **inside address**

City, State   Zip Code

Person(s) or Business Name: **greeting or salutation**

_____

                    body

_____

_____

_____

                    closing   Appropriate closing,

                                    Written Signature

                    signature   Typed Signature

There are many acceptable business letter formats; this is only one.

BUSINESS LETTER

<u>**Sample:**</u>

11124 South Drake Drive

Anaheim, California   92827

May 20, 2067

Bristo Enterprises

P. O. Box 35

Phoenix, Arizona   85032

Ladies and Gentlemen:

    Last March I ordered several items from your catalog: a red wagon (#LD 2437),

a deck of cards (#SP 1030), and a revolving flashlight (#FL 5550).   I also enclosed

a personal check for the total of the three items: check number 321, City Bank,

amount - $46.23.   I have not received my goods.   Please ship them immediately.

Sincerely yours,

Laura P. Belts

Laura P. Belts

ENVELOPE

The envelope for a friendly letter and a business letter are the same. The block style is shown here; block style means that each line is exactly below the preceding line.

YOUR NAME   * * * * * * * * *

NUMBER AND STREET ADDRESS   **return address**   STAMP

CITY, STATE   ZIP CODE   * * * * * * * * *

PERSON TO WHOM YOU ARE SENDING LETTER*

NUMBER AND STREET NAME

CITY, STATE   ZIP CODE

---

*or company

Ted Kline   * * * * * * * * *

2265 Morningstar Lane   STAMP

Gettysburg, Pennsylvania 17325   * * * * * * * * *

Miss Susan Smith

712 Tabby Lane

Phoenix, Arizona 85308

PREPOSITION TEST

Directions: Cross out any prepositional phrases. Underline the subject once and the verb/verb phrase twice.

1.   One of the men leaned against the door during the discussion.

2.   Several dogs at the veterinarian's office were lying by their owners' feet.

3.   Kerry stood in the rain and waited along with the other bus riders.

4.   After the accident, a policeman walked toward the damaged car.

5.   Claude and his aunt live near the park on Houston Avenue.

6.   Before the school carnival, many students carried chairs into a tent.

7.   His nearest neighbor lives across the field and past some water tanks.

8.   Please place this poster regarding water safety above the door.

9.   You may not go outside without your coat, hat, and boots.

10.   Throughout the spring, nine robins played underneath our willow tree.

11.   A model stood among the ladies and instructed them about proper nutrition.

12.   Some horses were running around in the field between the barn and the house.

13.   Everyone but the tall man in the blue wool suit remained for the banquet.

14.   After the meeting, Mom and her friend will help with refreshments until nine o'clock.

15.   Large dogs like shepherds and retrievers aren't allowed within the gated area.

Name_____ **VERB TEST**

Date_____

A. Directions: Write each contraction.

1. they will - _____

2. I am - _____

3. it is - _____

4. was not - _____

5. you are - _____

6. she would - _____

7. could not - _____

8. will not - _____

9. they are - _____

10. you will - _____

11. she is - _____

12. do not - _____

13. I shall - _____

14. cannot - _____

15. we are - _____

16. is not - _____

17. who is - _____

18. does not - _____

19. here is - _____

20. I have - _____

21. are not - _____

22. we are - _____

B. Directions: Circle the correct verb.

1. Juan has (saw, seen) the Hope Diamond.

2. She (teached, taught) us how to dive properly.

3. The balls were (thrown, threw) into the center of the ring.

4. This mop has been (shook, shaken) several times.

5. Her mother must have (come, came) by to see her today.

6. Herbs were (grown, grew) in a box on the window sill.

7. The Harrison family may have (went, gone) water skiing.

8. They should have (rode, ridden) their bikes in the rain.

9. Jenny has (swam, swum) since her first birthday.

10. Have you ever (broke, broken) a bone?

C.   Directions: Circle the correct verb.

1.   Have you (laid, lain) on the bed very long?

2.   If you would have asked, I would have (gave, given) you a key.

3.   Each of the choir members has (sung, sang) a solo this year.

4.   Was the fireman (took, taken) to the hospital for smoke inhalation?

5.   Several of the bubbles had (burst, bursted) on the wand.

6.   His answers were (written, wrote) in black ink.

7.   The welder has (brung, brought) two torches with him.

8.   His mother may have (spoke, spoken) to the coach about his injury.

9.   Many hot dogs were (ate, eaten) by the hungry hikers.

10.   The candle must have been (blew, blown) out.

11.   I should have (risen, rose) earlier than nine o'clock.

12.   Sandy could not have (drunk, drank) another ounce of soda.

13.   That racer has (ran, run) the mile faster than his opponents.

14.   That traveler will have (driven, drove) a thousand miles by the end of her trip.

15.   All of the towels were (shook, shaken) and placed on the line to dry.

16.   Have the boys and girls (done, did) the scenery for the play?

17.   George Washington was (swore, sworn) into office in New York City.

18.   This jacket must have (fell, fallen) on the dirty cement.

19.   Many pizzas had been (froze, frozen) for the victory celebration.

20.   Octopi are (known, knew) by their long, slender tentacles.

21.   The baseball player had (stole, stolen) home during the last inning.

22.   The Eastern team had (beat, beaten) the Western one in the playoffs.

23.   Her jacket had been (torn, tore) by a bush with large thorns.

24.   A lady has (bought, boughten) several ceramic giraffes.

25.   Their family has (went, gone) to the circus.

D.   Directions: Circle the verb that agrees with the subject.

1.   Sponges (is, are) a type of invertebrates.

2.   A few loons (swim, swims) on that lake each day.

3.   A kindergartner (walk, walks) with her father to school each day.

4.   Each of the divers (perform, performs) three dives in the competition.

5.   Several ranchers (meets, meet) each week to discuss plans for a town barbecue.

6.   A woman with a pretty smile (greet, greets) us at church each week.

7.   Pam's grandfathers (builds, build) vacation cabins in the mountains.

8.   Everyone of the club members (attend, attends) at least three meetings a year.

9.   Freda or her mother (take, takes) the dog for a walk each morning.

E.   Directions: Cross out any prepositional phrases. Underline the subject once the verb/verb phrase twice. In the space provided, write the tense: *present, past, future, present perfect, past perfect, future perfect, present progressive, past progressive,* or *future progressive.*

1.   _____   The boys were yelling to their friends.

2.   _____   Patrick hit the baseball past second base.

3.   _____   One carpenter had forgotten his tools.

4.   _____   By March, she will have saved twenty dollars.

5.   _____   Has anyone brought a drink for the picnic?

6.   _____   A dance student is buying new ballet shoes.

7.   _____   Their brother plays in a sandbox daily.

8.   _____   Will those senators be meeting next week?

9.   _____   Miss Lee will make a decision about moving.

F.   Directions: Cross out any prepositional phrases. Underline the subject
                    once and the verb/verb phrase twice.   Label any direct object-D.O.

1.   Her dog is (sitting, setting) by her mother.

2.   Have you (laid, lain) this blanket here?

3.   Each person (rose, raised) his hand to vote.

4.   Is the cat (lying, laying) near the litter box?

5.   A toddler (lay, laid) down on a couch to sleep.

6.   Miss Stark (raises, rises) late on Saturdays.

7.   (Sit, Set) this plate on the table.

8.   Everyone in the arena (rose, raised) to sing the national anthem.

9.   (Sit, Set) in the last row.

G.   Directions: Cross out any prepositional phrases.   Underline the subject once
                    and the verb/verb phrase twice. In the space provided, write L if
                    the verb is linking and A if the verb shows action.

1.   _____   Chris's hamster eats special food.

2.   _____   Bryan tasted some cheesy Greek pie.

3.   _____   Meredith bowled a nearly perfect game.

4.   _____   This bun became hard after three days.

5.   _____   Your fresh fudge seems too soft to cut.

6.   _____   Several children skated on a pond.

7.   _____   Joel became an engineer.

8.   _____   Mrs. Korb is staying with her mother.

9.   _____   The child seemed eager to learn to skate.

320

H.   Directions: Cross out any prepositional phrases. Underline the subject once
      and the verb/verb phrase twice. Write the helping (auxiliary) verb(s)
      in the first column and the main verb in the second column.

	HELPING VERB(S)	MAIN VERB

1.   I shall find a way.   _____ _____

2.   Should Bo come with us?   _____ _____

3.   He may have gone to a baseball
      game.   _____ _____

4.   Several watermelons are lying
      near the fence in the garden.   _____ _____

5.   That booth was constructed by
      high school seniors.   _____ _____

6.   Someone in that city can win
      a trip to Alaska.   _____ _____

I.   Directions: Cross out any prepositional phrases. Underline the subject once
      and the verb/verb phrase twice.

1.   Mr. Swanson might be going to Canada soon.

2.   Have you taken your guitar to the music store for repair?

3.   Several rare birds had been seen within a few hours.

4.   Before the wedding, the groom must have become very nervous.

5.   One of the robins has built a nest in the pine tree.

6.   Connie will not be driving to her grandmother's house alone.

7.   Can you understand the problem between the two boys?

8.   Would you be interested in a ticket to an amusement park?

CUMULATIVE TEST
Verb Unit

Directions: Cross out any prepositional phrases. Underline the subject once
and the verb/verb phrase twice.

1. During the game's final seconds, a basketball player made a basket from mid-court.

2. Everyone of the hot air balloons rose early in the moist morning.

3. The horse and its rider continued to meander down the dusty road.

4. Many bats had flown out of the cave after the storm at sundown.

5. Beyond that mountain is a lush green valley about ten square miles in area.

6. All calves but the one near its mother ambled over to the fence.

7. Kathryn cannot go to the beach without sunblock and her beach umbrella.

8. Clay's paper concerning rabies has been placed underneath some books on his desk.

9. Toward the end of the tour, the choir will be traveling through small Swiss villages.

10. Mrs. Kempler and her son ski before dinner nearly every day except Sunday.

11. In the lot across from the park, several volunteers planted flowers among some tall trees.

12. Please place these within the manila envelopes and address them, too.

13. Throughout the game, the goalie does not play beyond that point.

14. The statue inside the new history museum looks like their Uncle Anthony.

15. The small jet took off within ten minutes of its arrival at Scottsdale Airport.

Name_____ **NOUN TEST**

Date_____

A. Directions: Write <u>C</u> if the word is a concrete noun; write <u>A</u> if the word is an abstract noun.

1. _____ wisdom   3. _____ air   5. _____ happiness
2. _____ lion   4. _____ shutter   6. _____ microscope

B. Write <u>C</u> for common; write <u>P</u> for proper.

1. _____ AIRPLANE   4. _____ ADAMS COUNTY

2. _____ JET   5. _____ WASHINGTON, D.C.

3. _____ SOUTHWEST AIRLINES 6. _____ SKATER

C. Directions: Write <u>N</u> if the boldfaced word serves as a noun; write <u>A</u> if the boldfaced word serves as an adjective. Write <u>V</u> if the boldfaced word serves as a verb.

1. _____ Does she **park** her car there every night?
2. _____ In the spring, the residents enjoy the **park**.
3. _____ Those **park** lights are too bright.
4. _____ "I'd like **cream** for my coffee," said Mr. Post.
5. _____ To make these cookies, **cream** butter and sugar together first.
6. _____ A white **cream** sauce is used as a base for this soup.

D. Directions: Write the possessive and the word it owns.

1. a computer belonging to Vincent: _____

2. skis belonging to three girls: _____

3. a restroom for more than one man: _____

4. brushes belonging to James: _____

5. a project belonging to two students: _____

323

Directions: In the space provided, write <u>PN</u> if the boldfaced noun serves as a predicate nominative, <u>D.O.</u> if the boldfaced noun serves as a direct object, and <u>I.O.</u> if the boldfaced noun serves as an indirect object. If the noun serves as an appositive, write <u>APP.</u> in the space.

1. _____ The first shape on the page is a **triangle**.
2. _____ Mr. Carlson, his soccer **coach**, talked to the team about sportsmanship.
3. _____ Marge always sends post **cards** to her cousin.
4. _____ The tailor made **Fred** a pin-striped suit.
5. _____ The third United States President was **Jefferson**.
6. _____ Please take your **belongings** with you.
7. _____ Trish handed the mail **lady** a large envelope.

F. Directions: Write the plural of each noun.

1. crepe - _____
2. octopus - _____
3. crash - _____
4. fez - _____

5. decoy - _____
6. berry - _____
7. cross - _____
8. branch - _____

G. Directions: First, circle any determiner in the sentence. Then, box any noun following a determiner. Next, reread the sentence and box any other noun(s) in the sentence.

1. Some bats will be flying from that cave after sundown.

2. Has Earl's cousin purchased a brick home across from the new library?

3. The ladies' club gave two scholarships to those women returning for a college degree.

4. No money was given to my sister for an expedition to Africa in the spring.

5. Our grandmother is known for her wisdom concerning many matters.

6. Their family went to Lake Powell, a beautiful body of water in northern Arizona.

7. Todd and I watched a monkey chase its partner.

A. Directions: Cross out any prepositional phrases. Underline the subject once
                 and the verb/verb phrase twice.

1. All band members, but William and Iva, will be playing in the concert.

2. A huge basket of flowers has been placed upon the dining room table.

3. Keep your shoes with the rubber soles in the laundry room.

4. During the storm, a group of children stayed inside to play.

5. Gregg and I planted flowers between a low wall and our house.

B. Directions: Write the contraction.

1. I have - _____   3. what is - _____   5. I would - _____

2 could not - _____   4. they are - _____   6. will not - _____

C. Directions: Write L if the verb is linking; write A if the verb is action.

1. _____ The cook tastes all of her soups.

2. _____ After the lights went out, we felt our way down the hallway.

3. _____ Mrs. Fox has become a business owner.

4. _____ In January, the weather is usually very cold.

D. Directions: Write the correct form of the verb in the space provided.

(to break)   1. Her wrist had been _____ in the fall.

(to take)   2. Lasagna _____ much time to prepare.

(to hang)   3. Several trousers were _____ in the closet.

(to ride)   4. He has _____ his horse for an hour.

(to swim)   5.   The athlete had _____ the English Channel.

(to be)   6.   Your behavior has _____ outstanding.

(to drink)   7.   Several gallons of water had been _____ by the thirsty workers.

(to talk)   8.   Both the coach and her assistant often _____ with the team.

(to come)   9.   Several surfers had _____ to the beach before dawn.

(to go)   10.   Jim and Annie had _____ to a car derby.

(to send)   11.   That company _____ catalogs to its customers.

(to lie)   12.   Many beach visitors had _____ quietly watching the ocean.

E.   Directions: Cross out any prepositional phrases. Underline the subject once and the verb/verb phrase twice. On the space provided, write the tense: *present, past, future, present perfect, past perfect, future perfect, present progressive, past progressive,* or *future progressive.*

1.   _____   I am waiting for the next bus.

2.   _____   The letter from Aunt Sue arrived before noon.

3.   _____   Those boots are in great shape.

4.   _____   By the end of the month, he will have written forty checks.

F.   Directions: Cross out any prepositional phrases. Underline the subject once and the verb/verb phrase twice.

1.   A petition concerning zoning was passed around the neighborhood.

2.   I shall not have to leave until Wednesday.

3.   Go toward your opponent but move outside his reach.

4.   This plate should have been placed under the fancy saucers.

5.   Are the travelers going through many tunnels during their time in Switzerland?

Name_____   **ADJECTIVE TEST**

Date_____

A. Directions: Write the proper adjective and the noun it modifies in the space
provided.

1. Have you been to a maryland beach?   _____

2. Jacob wants a magnavox television.   _____

3. Do you like carnation chocolate milk?   _____

4. A platter of french toast was served.   _____

5. "I enjoy mexican food," said Brett.   _____

6. Sue's choir is planning a european tour.   _____

7. Some hawaiian sunsets are colorful.   _____

B. Directions: Write the predicate adjective and the noun it modifies in the space
provided. If there is no predicate adjective in the sentence, write
none on the line.

1. The head nurse appears upset.   _____

2. Your antique quilt looks new.   _____

3. These stones feel sharp to my feet.   _____

4. Her gift was a beautiful red shawl.   _____

5. The girl remained calm during her speech. _____

6. This lemon pie tastes quite tangy.   _____

7. The picnickers remained in a quiet spot.   _____

8. A worker grew tired in the midday heat.   _____

C. Directions: Choose the correct adjective form.

1. Mt. Everest is (taller, tallest) than Mt. Fuji.

2. Is Lake Superior the (deeper, deepest) lake in the world?

3. Austrid is the (more intelligent, most intelligent) person I know.

4. Was your rafting trip the (more daring, most daring) one you've ever taken?

5. Mrs. Parks is the (nicer, nicest) of the two helpers.

6. Which of these three worms is (longer, longest)?

7. The wedding cake chosen by Cynthia was (larger, largest) than the one selected by her fiance.

D. Directions: Circle any adjectives.

Suggestion: Read each sentence carefully. Circle any limiting adjectives. Then, circle any descriptive adjectives.

1. Two warm bran muffins and orange juice were part of the appetizing breakfast.

2. This tall street light with pink frosted panes serves as an easy landmark.

3. Has Jerome's great uncle visited the covered bridges of the New England states?

4. A cream-filled chocolate eclair with whipped cream topping was the main dessert.

5. Sarah's youngest son had ridden his mountain bike on that spring outing.

6. Several small children were petting a few comical, fluffy puppies.

7. These were the warmest leather boots in the entire shoe store.

8. An American flag was flying at their local post office.

9. Our favorite restaurant is a Chinese one in lower Manhattan.

10. Many flowering cherry trees bloom each year in our nation's capital.

Name_____

Date_____

A. Directions: Fill in the blank.

1. An example of an abstract noun is _____.

2. An example of a common noun is _____.

3. An example of an interjection is _____.

4. An example of a proper adjective is _____.

5. A word that ends a prepositional phrase is called an _____.

B. Directions: Write the plural of the following nouns.

1. cinch - _____   4. burglar - _____   7. buoy - _____

2. fungus - _____   5. grocery - _____   8. ox - _____

3. paste - _____   6. starfish - _____   9. sister-in-law - _____

C. Directions: Write the contraction.

1. she is - _____   3. cannot - _____   5. you are - _____

2. should not - _____   4. is not - _____   6. had not - _____

D. Directions: Write A if the boldfaced word serves as an adjective; write N if the boldfaced word serves as a noun. Write V if the boldfaced word serves as a verb.

1. _____ This **light** fixture is dirty.

2. _____ Please turn on a **light**.

3. _____ Please **light** the candles.

4. _____ Janice **skates** on her neighbor's pond.

5. _____ Place those **skates** in the closet.

E.   Directions: Write fifty prepositions.

1. _____   14. _____   27. _____   40. _____

2. _____   15. _____   28. _____   41. _____

3. _____   16. _____   29. _____   42. _____

4. _____   17. _____   30. _____   43. _____

5. _____   18. _____   31. _____   44. _____

6. _____   19. _____   32. _____   45. _____

7. _____   20. _____   33. _____   46. _____

8. _____   21. _____   34. _____   47. _____

9. _____   22. _____   35. _____   48. _____

10. _____   23. _____   36. _____   49. _____

11. _____   24. _____   37. _____   50. _____

12. _____   25. _____   38. _____

13. _____   26. _____   39. _____

F.   Directions: Cross out any prepositional phrases. Underline the subject once
                   and the verb/verb phrase twice. Label any direct object -D.O.; label
                   any indirect object - I.O.

1.   Everyone of the girls on the softball team must carry her own equipment.

2.   Frank and his best friend will be going to Baltimore and Annapolis in the spring.

3.   Please give your mother this recipe for hot cross buns.

4.   Throughout the year, several girls met at Mrs. Polk's house to discuss field day.

5.   Has your dentist given you information about a new type of toothbrush?
330

G. Directions: Write the correct verb form in the space provided.

(to choose) 1. Has the group _____ its leader?

(to do) 2. The dishes must be _____ soon.

(to sink) 3. Her toes have _____ into the mud.

(to ring) 4. The tardy bell had _____.

(to see) 5. You should have _____ the look on his face.

(to give) 6. We were _____ several mush balls.

(to drink) 7. Have you ever _____ mineral water?

(to take) 8. Campaign posters were _____ down immediately after the election.

(to bring) 9. Jack has _____ along his dog.

(to part) 10. Whitney had _____ her hair in the middle.

H. Directions: Circle the correct possessive:

1. Several (lady's, ladies') hats were on sale.
2. The (children's, childrens') playground is rather small.
3. One (boy's, boys') picture had been hung on the wall.
4. An award was presented to the (city's, citys') mayor.
5. Some (wasp's, wasps') hives were in a palm tree.

I. Directions: Circle any adjectives.

Suggestion: First, circle any limiting adjective(s) in a sentence. Then, circle any descriptive adjective(s).

1. That triangle has three equal sides.
2. A few dogs with pretty bows on their ears left the groomer's work area.
3. Sixteen tourists rode a double-decker bus through several London streets.
4. A small, furry animal darted in front of their speeding car.

J. Directions: Write the tense of the verb in the space provided.

(present of *to eat*)   1. This hamster _____ very little.

(future of *to fly*)   2. We _____ a kite on a windy day.

(past perfect of *to*   3. Jonah _____ early.
    learn)

(present progressive   4. Nelly _____ to a gym.
   of *to go*)

K. Directions: Box any nouns.

Suggestion: Identifying adjectives helps to locate most nouns.

1. An unusual computer is sitting on a card table in the middle of their kitchen.

2. In most cases, that attorney speaks to his new client in a private office.

3. In Germany, my father and I visited one castle, several vineyards, and a lake.

4. Will you help Mr. Kirk with this bushel of apples and those sacks of potatoes?

L. Directions: Write APP. if the boldfaced noun serves as an appositive, D.O. if the
                boldfaced word serves as a direct object, and PN if the boldfaced
                word serves as a predicate nominative.

1. _____ I have lost a coin, a **dime**.
2. _____ The winner of a free basket of goodies is **Mrs. Larkins**.
3. _____ Throughout the day, the dog chewed his new **bone**.
4. _____ Give Jason a **copy** of that advertisement.

M. Directions: Circle the correct verb.

1. Several chickens (live, lives) in that barn.
2. A customer (sat, set) her purse on the glass counter.
3. The child (lay, laid) on his stomach to watch television.
4. Benny's aunt and uncle (work, works) at a grocery store.
5. Neither my mother nor my sisters (want, wants) another cat.
332

A. Directions: Write the adverb form of each word.

1. easy -   _____

2. foolish -   _____

3. nervous -   _____

4. fast -   _____

5. final -   _____

6. sudden -   _____

7. good -   _____

8. recent -   _____

B. Directions: Cross out any prepositional phrases.   Underline the subject once
                 and verb/verb phrase twice. Circle any adverbs.

1. Quickly he grabbed the fire extinguisher from above the fireplace.

2. Please remove the tiles in the family room very carefully.

3. Shanna hit the ball hard during her first practice.

4. A waitress usually works fast during dinner hour.

5. You can swim underneath the water so well.

6. He answered all questions courteously and confidently.

7. We need to work together on this project concerning recycling.

8. A plumber could not come immediately.

9. You are always quite friendly and act agreeably.

10. One of the penguins padded quite swiftly to the water's edge.

C. Directions: Write **good** or **well** in the space provided.

1. His exams went _____.

2. This is a _____ way to tie a double knot.

3. You are doing _____; keep it up!

4. Miss Jansen doesn't feel _____ today.

5. Oprah swims very _____ for a beginner.

D. Directions: Circle the correct answer.

1. This frisbee flies (gooder, better) than that one.

2. Of the triplets, Tiffany sings (more beautifully, most beautifully).

3. Sweeping the kitchen takes (longer, longest) of all the chores.

4. My sister walks (more slowly, most slowly) to school than from school.

5. Jana hits the ball (harder, hardest) of the entire team.

6. To avoid a collision, the first car stopped (more abruptly, most abruptly) of the four.

E. Directions: Circle the correct answer.

1. Mark doesn't have (no, any) ride to the store.

2. I don't want (any, none).

3. Kenneth has (no, any) hobby.

4. She scarcely has (any, no) time to play.

5. The hamster hardly eats (anything, nothing).

6. You never want (anybody, nobody) to help you.
334

A. Directions: Circle any abstract noun.

      fin   fan   fist   fun   friend   female   fort   fence   faith   freedom

B. Directions: Write the plural of each noun.

1. proof - _____   4. calf - _____   7. mother-in-law_____

2. ash - _____   5. tissue - _____   8. derby - _____

3. ploy - _____   6. tooth - _____

C. Directions: Write the contraction.

1. should not - _____   3. it is - _____   5. they are - _____

2. we will - _____   4. you are - _____   6. I would - _____

D. Directions: Write <u>A</u> if the boldfaced word serves as an adjective; write <u>V</u> if the bold
                    faced word serves as a verb. Write <u>N</u> if the boldfaced word serves as
                    a noun.

1. _____ She attended a **flute** recital.

2. _____ Is the **flute** an expensive instrument?

3. _____ Did you **flute** the edges of the pie?

E. Directions: Cross out any prepositional phrases. Underline the subject once and
                    the verb/verb phase twice. Label any direct object-<u>D.O.</u> Label any
                    indirect object-<u>I.O.</u>

1. Most of the guests signed the register.

2. At the end of the seminar, books were sold at various booths.

3. Kelly baked the class brownies for her birthday.

F. Directions: Cross out any prepositional phrases. Underline the subject once and the verb/verb phrase twice.

1. Kimberly wouldn't ride her horse in the rodeo parade.

2. After sunrise, a group of men played golf for several hours.

3. Those ladies and their sons will be attending a banquet at our church.

4. Take these along with you, and wear them after your shower.

G. Directions: If the boldfaced noun serves as an appositive, write APP. in the space. If the boldfaced noun serves as a direct object, write D.O. in the space. If the boldfaced noun serves as a predicate nominative, write PN in the space.

Remember: You need a proof for a predicate nominative.

1. _____   Their cousin, **Ella**, attends a junior college.

2. _____   Our new neighbor is **Adam Jones**.

3. _____   The car door hit **Frankie** in the back.

H. Directions: Fill in the blank.

1. Write a proper noun.   _____

2. Write a proper adjective.   _____

3. Write a phrase.   _____

I. Directions: Write the sentence type.

1. _____   Where have you put the stapler?

2. _____   My answer is final.

3. _____   Please stop that.

4. _____   The train is moving!

J. Directions: Circle the correct adjective form.

1. This is the (funnier, funniest) show I have seen.

2. Jody's published copy was (better, best) than her rough draft.

3. Her reaction was (more pleasant, pleasanter) than I expected.

4. Of all the science projects, yours was the (more interesting, most interesting).

5. Of the triplets, Julie is (more creative, most creative).

K. Directions: Circle the correct verb.

1. The policeman (rose, raised) his hand to tell the driver to stop.

2. One of the truckers (wear, wears) a blue uniform.

3. Have you (chose, chosen) a different route for the detour?

4. The baby may have (drank, drunk) a full six ounces of milk.

5. A bracelet is (laying, lying) on the floor.

6. Has the chemist (gave, given) us the test results?

7. Few workers (is, are) taking a break early.

8. We should have (brought, brang) our jackets.

9. The jurist must have (took, taken) a newspaper along.

10. One of the dogs (eat, eats) the other's food.

11. The key chain and an extra key (was, were) on the desk.

12. A visitor must have been (sitting, setting) in that empty seat.

13. Have you ever (wrote, written) your name backwards?

14. (Lie, Lay) your tiles for the board game on the table.

15. Mr. and Mrs. Dobson (leaves, leave) early each morning.

L.   Directions: Write the possessive form.

1.   a yard sale belonging to two families - _____

2.   notes belonging to a speaker - _____

3.   a clothing store for more than one man - _____

M.   Directions: Circle any adjectives.

1.   Several blue helium balloons are attached to that long metal pole.

N.   Directions: Box any nouns.

1.   I must take two boxes of mystery books to the library during the afternoon.

O.   Directions: Write P if the group of words is a phrase; write C if the group of words
          is a clause.
1.   _____   Down the street.   3.   _____   Running through the hall.
2.   _____   After James left.   4.   _____   Claude has a new hamster.

P.   Directions: Write the tense.

1.   _____   His grandfather goes to bed early.
2.   _____   Have you washed your hair today?
3.   _____   Are you planning a surprise party?

Q.   Directions: Write S if the group of words is a sentence. Write F if the group of
          words is a fragment. Write R-O if the group of words is a run-on.
1.   _____   The batter struck out, but he ran to first base anyway.
2.   _____   Melinda rides to the store, her friend always walks.
3.   _____   Driving a truck to pick up a load of hay.

R.   Directions: Fill in the blank.

1.   **Wow! We almost won!** What part of speech is <u>Wow!</u>? _____

2.   **Are you chewing gum?** The verb phrase is _____. The

     main verb is _____.

3.   **The little boy and girl painted Peter a picture.** Peter is the _____
338

Name_____   **PRONOUN TEST**

Date_____

A. Directions: Circle the correct pronoun.

1. (Who, Whom) wants to ride a roller coaster?

2. The managers are (them, they) standing by the door.

3. A chef gave (us, we) a lesson in chopping food.

4. (Me, I) intend to explore a cave soon.

5. Her friend writes to (her, she) nearly every week.

6. May (we, us) boys play now?

7. This discussion will remain between you and (I, me).

8. To (who, whom) did you give a hamburger?

9. Our dentist gives (we, us) patients a toothbrush.

10. The librarian told (he, him) to work more quietly.

B. Directions: Write P in the blank if the boldfaced word serves as a pronoun;
              write A in the blank if the boldfaced word serves as an adjective.

1. _____   **Which** do you want?

2. _____   Are **those** yours?

3. _____   **What** time is it?

4. _____   **That** golf cart is broken.

5. _____   **Each** must carry his own gear.

C. Directions: Circle the correct word.

1. (Their, They're) dog is loose again.

2. I believe (you're, your) right!

3. (It's, Its) going to be very cloudy today.

4. A turtle turned (it's, its) head slowly from side to side.

5. Please ask if (their, they're) dad is coming to get them.

D.   Directions: Circle the correct pronoun.

1.   Madge gave Shanna and (he, him) several popsicles.

2.   Judy and (I, me) noticed a flaw in the sweater.

3.   Both want (his, their) dinners late.

4.   The explorers and (we, us) want to visit Carlsbad Caverns.

5.   Harry and (they, them) might be going to Acapulco.

6.   The last people chosen were Karen and (we, us).

E.   Directions: Write the antecedent of the boldfaced word.

1.   _____   A small insect spread **its** wings.

2.   _____   Marcus's farm set is **his** favorite toy.

3.   _____   The men looked at **their** boss's schedule to determine if they had to work on Tuesday.

4.   _____   One of the boys left **his** books.

5.   _____   Joanna and her mother love **their** exercise machines.

F.   Directions: Tell how the boldfaced pronoun functions in the sentence.

   A. subject   B. direct object   C. indirect object
   D. object of the preposition   E. predicate nominative

1. _____   The first person to arrive at the restaurant was **he**.
2. _____   **They** fly kites on windy days.
3. _____   A bakery made **us** a beautiful orange cake.
4. _____   A lady in charge handed **me** several T-shirts.
5. _____   Has **she** cleaned her carpets?
6. _____   Did **you** understand the directions?
7. _____   A referee threw **him** out of the game.

340

A.   Directions: Write <u>PN</u> in the space if the boldfaced word serves as a predicate nominative.   Write <u>PA</u> if the boldfaced word serves as a predicate adjective.   Write <u>NO</u> if the boldfaced word does not serve as a predicate nominative or predicate adjective.

1.   _____   Your hands look very **chapped**.

2.   _____   Miss Liston is my friend's **aunt**.

3.   _____   Fran looks for **money** with her metal detector.

4.   _____   This **old** coin was used in ancient Rome.

5.   _____   My best friend is **she** in the blue dress.

B.   Directions: Circle the correct adverb form.

1.   My sister doesn't ever drive (slow, slowly).

2.   That first grader writes her name (good, well).

3.   The children playing in the water yelled (loud, loudly) to the passing boat driver.

4.   His voice rose (sharp, sharply) as he became angrier.

C.   Directions: Circle any adverbs.

1.   We sometimes go there for lunch.

2.   How did you hurt your wrist so badly?

3.   A race horse galloped swiftly by.

4.   The lady has frantically searched everywhere for the missing money.

5.   He dashed in, looked down at his shoes, and began to chuckle softly.

D.   Directions: Label any conjunction-<u>Conj</u>.; label any interjection-<u>Intj</u>.

1.   Yippee!   Mark and Mandy are entering the race!

2.   Either Holly or her sister attends college in North Carolina.

3.   Hurray!   My parents are going to the reunion, but I may go fishing!

E. Directions: Write the sentence type.

1. _____ Stand up.

2. _____ Look at him stand on his head!

3. _____ He is standing on his head.

4. _____ Can you stand on your head?

F. Directions: Write the tense: *present, past, future, present perfect, past perfect, future perfect, present progressive, past progressive, future progressive.*

1. _____ She likes tarantulas.

2. _____ I shall be flying to Denver next month.

3. _____ The child has fallen off a swing.

4. _____ By spring, Ted will have taken all his exams.

5. _____ Mayor Loo greeted the ambassador from Peru.

6. _____ A newspaper was lying by the road.

G. Directions: Write the contraction.

1. I am - _____   3. will not - _____   5. there is - _____

2. you are - _____   4. we are - _____   6. they have - _____

H. Directions: Write A if the noun is abstract; write C if the noun is concrete.

1. ___ kindness   2. ___ salad   3. ___ caution   4. ___ harp   5. ___ joy

I. Directions: Write C if the noun is common; write P if the noun is proper.

1. ___ PLANT   2. ___ GRASS   3. ___ TOWER   4. ___ EIFFEL TOWER

5. ___ OREGON 6. ___ AMERICA 7. ___ ANGEL   8. ___ GABRIEL

342

J. Directions: Write <u>D.O.</u> if the boldfaced word serves as a direct object.
Write <u>I.O.</u> if the boldfaced word serves as an indirect object.
Write <u>AP</u>. if the boldfaced word serves as an appositive.

1. _____ Dad handed **Tammy** an apple for her lunch.

2. _____ Their friend, **Tammy**, is a great seminar speaker.

3. _____ A small child hit **Tammy** on the back with a toy.

K. Directions: Cross out any prepositional phrases. Underline the subject once and
the verb/verb phrase twice.

1. Several of the crew members took a break and sat in the shade.

2. A lion with his ears at attention is lying between two trees near a stream.

3. Take this sword to the auditorium for Miss Dormal and Mr. Master.

4. Headlights should have been turned on before the tunnel entrance.

5. Haven't you ever walked through the woods on a cold, crisp winter day?

L. Directions: Circle the correct answer.

1. A (childrens', children's) play area has been added.

2. Has Uncle Marty done that (himself, hisself)?

3. Several (boy's, boys') jackets are on sale.

4. One (lamb's, lambs') mouth seems to be sore.

5. (You're, Your) idea is being considered.

6. Many (skiers', skier's) poles have been slightly bent.

7. (Mrs. Hass, Mrs. Hass's) husband is an orthodontist.

8. The peacock was spreading (it's, its) beautiful tail.

9. Sooner or later, the (women's, womens') club must reach a decision.

M. Directions: Write the plural.

1. lotus - _____

2. nursery - _____

3. clay - _____

4. leaf - _____

5. pitch - _____

6. son-in-law - _____

7. laughter - _____

8. circle - _____

N. Directions: Circle each correct answer.

1. The parade had not (came, come) down the main street.

2. This opening is (narrower, narrowest) of the three.

3. Nancy's grandmother (serves, serve) as our church's greeter.

4. (You're, Your) the person I most respect.

5. The police officer has (rode, ridden) a horse on his beat for several years.

6. The lady with those crying children (is, are) very upset.

7. The man scrubbed the floor (more vigorously, most vigorously) the second time.

8. A zebra and a giraffe often (stand, stands) near a tree in the African meadow.

9. Two year olds frequently want to do things (theirselves, themselves).

10. Have you (brang, brought) a suitcase with you?

11. (Lie, Lay) here beside the fire and get warm.

12. He (sits, sets) under a tree in the park nearly every evening.

13. The pilot must have (went, gone) to the airport already.

14. This matter is between your sister and (I, me).

15. Her father must have (laid, lain) in his recliner all afternoon.

16. Give (we, us) adults a chance to help you.

17. The winner should have been (me, I).

18. Many ribbons have been given to (her, she) for her athletic talent.

19. Everyone must take (their, his) clothes into the laundry room.

20. Several people in the overturned boat had (swam, swum) to the river's bank.

21. When the phone rang, he answered, "This is (he, him)."

22. The light fixture had been (broke, broken) while still in the box.

23. (We, Us) will be meeting with a senator from Kansas.

24. You are much taller than (I, me).

O.   Directions: Box any nouns.

1.   The desert is a habitat for some snakes and various cacti.

2.   I need a package of napkins, some paper plates, and a few straws for our picnic.

3.   Lee's aunt is an aspiring violinist; she hopes to play with the Phoenix Symphony.

4.   These boxes containing two lamps were sent to the girls' apartment by mistake.

P.   Directions: Circle any adjectives.

1.   Several beautiful models wore soft, flowing dresses made of imported silk.

2.   Five Dalmatian puppies scampered friskily among many shrubs on their back lawn.

3.   The Irish countryside is fertile, very green, and scenic in the summer.

4.   That man writes funny short stories, Gothic novels, and humorous poetry.

Q.   Directions: Read each group of words. Write F for fragment, S for sentence, and
                   R-O for run-on.

1.   _____   Having been chosen as the best.
2.   _____   Jenny and John have been married a year.
3.   _____   Pizza was delivered for dinner, unfortunately, it was cold.
4.   _____   During the summer, Brian goes to his grandmother and grandfather's
               house in Nebraska and loves swimming in a creek by their home and
               going to the local fairs plus he drives the tractor on their farm.

R.   Directions: Circle the correct answer.

1.   They feel (happy, happily) about their choice.
2.   You painted that wall (quick, quickly).
3.   Garth does his job (good, well).
4.   Kimberly's mother looks (tired, tiredly) today.
5.   He answered the question (weird, weirdly).
6.   Of the four sandwiches, the beef one was (more delicious, most delicious).

Name_____

Date_____

Directions: Insert needed punctuation.

1. Gails dad lives at 17251 N Palomino Avenue Sedalia CO 80135

2. Edna hasnt your family visited Trafalgar Square Green Park and Barclay Square in London

3. Her father in law is that tall talkative man in the gray jacket said Mrs Somerset

4. Bernard Waber wrote a childrens book entitled Ira Sleeps Over

5. Yuck The two dogs dishes are covered with bits of food and ants are crawling all over the bowls

6. Jason their best friend was born in St Louis Missouri on May 20 1982 at 2 00 PM

7.

5503 East Blair Lane
Peoria Arizona   85345
March 18 20--

Dear Artie

The following three will be traveling to summer camp in your van Joshua Peter and Jenny

Sincerely
Patty

8. When Sally went to a ranch for summer vacation she read and loved the poem entitled Stopping by Woods on a Snowy Evening by Robert Frost

9. Jackson Co
    89 W Marilyn Lane
    Metamora Illinois   61548

    Dear Miss Hanna

    Three fourths of the article entitled Ultrasound Toothbrushes was supposed to be continued on page forty five   However that part of the article was missing

Very truly yours
Martin S Treubell

Name_____ **CAPITALIZATION TEST**

Date_____

Directions: Write the capital letter above any word that needs to be capitalized.

1. when captain lovell and i visited the south, we saw the savannah river and the site of the battle of shiloh, a famous civil war area.

2. they learned spanish, computer science, and algebra I at a junior high school.

3. i. geographical locations
       a. rivers
       b. mountains
            1. located in europe
            2. located in north america

4. their methodist minister talked about king solomon and the book of <u>proverbs</u> during a father's day sermon.

5. juan and his polynesian friend attended a play entitled <u>he was with me in the den</u> at star theater last saturday.

6. a child with bronchitis was treated at sunset memorial hospital on drye lane.

7. did mayor torris drive across the golden gate bridge when visiting northern california last winter?

8. after buying several gifts at swan gift shop, the american tourist boarded a trans world airline flight for new york city.

9. "during thanksgiving vacation, mother and aunt jane helped the moon valley helpers club teach spanish at largent college," said ellen.

10.
                                    1882 south breck drive
                                    atlanta, georgia   30327
                                    january 4, 20--

    dear sally,

            to travel to grand canyon national park from your home, take the black canyon freeway to flagstaff, arizona, and turn west.

                                    your friend,
                                    anne

INDEX